Cambridge Latin Course

INTEGRATED EDITION

Unit IIIB

with Language Information

CAMBRIDGE
UNIVERSITY PRESS

PUBLISHED BY THE PRESS SYNDICATE OF THE UNIVERSITY OF CAMBRIDGE
The Pitt Building, Trumpington Street, Cambridge, United Kingdom

CAMBRIDGE UNIVERSITY PRESS
The Edinburgh Building, Cambridge CB2 2RU, UK
40 West 20th Street, New York, NY 10011–4211, USA
10 Stamford Road, Oakleigh, VIC 3166, Australia
Ruiz de Alarcón 13, 28014 Madrid, Spain
Dock House, The Waterfront, Cape Town 8001, South Africa

http://www.cambridge.org

This book, an outcome of work jointly commissioned by the Schools Council
before its closure and the Cambridge School Classics Project, is published under
the aegis of Qualifications and Curriculum Authority Enterprises Limited,
Newcombe House, 45 Notting Hill Gate, London W11 3JB

© Qualifications and Curriculum Authority Enterprises Limited 1971, 1984, 1990

First published 1971
Seventh printing 1982
Second edition 1984
Fifth printing 1988
Integrated edition 1990
Eleventh printing 2000

Printed in the United Kingdom at the University Press, Cambridge

ISBN 0 521 38949 6 paperback

Thanks are due to the following for permission to reproduce photogaphs:
pp 10, 12 from Yigael Yadin *Masada* and Weidenfeld and Nicolson Archives; p 21 Alinari;
pp 27, 33, 37, 73, 101, 102 The Mansell Collection; pp 40, 57, 59 Fototeca Unione, at the
American Academy in Rome; p 82 Museum of London; p 98 The Trustees of the British
Museum; p 120 Musee Royal de Mariemont. The publisher and author ask for the
forgiveness of those sources of illustrative material whose identity it proved impossible to
establish.

Drawings by Peter Kesteven, Joy Mellor and Leslie Jones.

Maps and diagrams by Reg Piggott and David Bryant.

Cover picture: Mosaic of two theatrical masks. (Musei Capitolini, Rome).

Contents

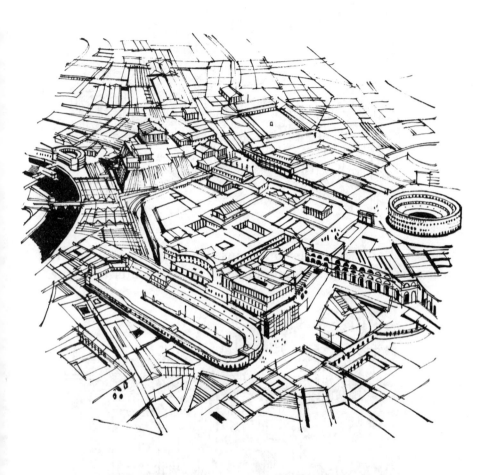

Rōma

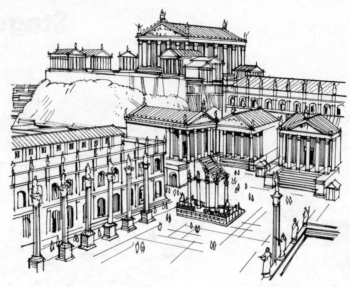

in mediā Rōmā est mōns nōtissimus, quī Capitōlium appellātur.
in summō Capitōliō stat templum, ubi deus Iuppiter adōrātur.

sub Capitōliō iacet forum Rōmānum.
forum ab ingentī multitūdine cīvium cotīdiē complētur.
aliī negōtium agunt; aliī in porticibus stant et ab amīcīs
salūtantur; aliī per forum in lectīcīs feruntur. ubīque magnus
strepitus audītur.

aliquandō pompae splendidae
per forum dūcuntur.

prope medium forum est
templum Vestae, ubi ignis sacer
ā Virginibus Vestālibus cūrātur.

in extrēmō forō stant Rōstra, ubi contiōnēs apud populum habentur.

prope Rōstra est carcer, ubi captīvī populī Rōmānī custōdiuntur.

nox

nox erat. lūna stēllaeque in caelō serēnō fulgēbant. tempus erat quō
hominēs quiēscere solent. Rōmae tamen nūlla erat quiēs, nūllum
silentium.

magnīs in domibus, ubi dīvitēs habitābant, cēnae splendidae
cōnsūmēbantur. cibus sūmptuōsus ā servīs offerēbātur; vīnum 5
optimum ab ancillīs fundēbātur; carmina ā citharoedīs perītissimīs
cantābantur.

in altīs autem īnsulīs, nūllae cēnae splendidae cōnsūmēbantur,
nūllī citharoedī audiēbantur. ibi pauperēs, famē paene cōnfectī,
vītam miserrimam agēbant. aliī ad patrōnōs epistulās scrībēbant ut 10
auxilium eōrum peterent, aliī scelera ac fūrta committere parābant.

prope forum magnus strepitus audiēbātur. nam arcus magnificus
in Viā Sacrā exstruēbātur. ingēns polyspaston arcuī imminēbat.
fabrī, quī arcum exstruēbant, dīligentissimē labōrābant. aliī figūrās
in arcū sculpēbant; aliī titulum in fronte arcūs īnscrībēbant; aliī 15
marmor ad summum arcum tollēbant. omnēs strēnuē labōrābant ut

serēnō: serēnus *calm, clear*
Rōmae *at Rome*
altīs: altus *high*
īnsulīs: īnsula *block of flats, apartment building*
famē: famēs *hunger*
cōnfectī: cōnfectus *worn out, exhausted*
patrōnōs: patrōnus *patron*
arcus *arch*
Viā Sacrā: Via Sacra *the Sacred Way (road running through forum)*
polyspaston *crane*
figūrās: figūra *figure, shape*
sculpēbant: sculpere *carve, model*
titulum: titulus *inscription*
fronte: frōns *front*
īnscrībēbant: īnscrībere *write, inscribe*
marmor *marble*

arcum ante lūcem perficerent. nam Imperātor Domitiānus hunc
arcum frātrī Titō postrīdiē dēdicāre volēbat. Titum vīvum ōderat;
mortuum tamen eum honōrāre cupiēbat. Domitiānus enim favōrem
populī Rōmānī, quī Titum maximē dīlēxerat, nunc sibi conciliāre 2(
volēbat.

praeerat huic operī Quīntus Haterius Latrōniānus, redēmptor
nōtissimus. eā nocte ipse fabrōs furēns incitābat. aderat quoque
Gāius Salvius Līberālis, Haterii patrōnus, quī eum invicem
flāgitābat ut opus ante lūcem perficeret. anxius enim erat Salvius 2!
quod Imperātōrī persuāserat ut Haterium operī praeficeret. ille
igitur fabrīs, quamquam omnīnō dēfessī erant, identidem imperāvit
nē labōre dēsisterent.

Glitus, magister fabrōrum, Haterium lēnīre temptābat.

'ecce, domine!' inquit. 'fabrī iam arcum paene perfēcērunt. 3(
ultimae litterae titulī nunc īnscrībuntur; ultimae figūrae
sculpuntur; ultimae marmoris massae ad summum arcum
tolluntur.'

paulō ante hōram prīmam, fabrī arcum tandem perfēcērunt;
abiērunt omnēs ut quiēscerent. paulīsper urbs silēbat.   3!

ūnus faber tamen, domum per forum rediēns, subitō trīstēs
fēminārum duārum clāmōrēs audīvit. duae enim captīvae, magnō
dolōre affectae, in carcere cantābant:

'mī Deus! mī Deus! respice mē! quārē mē dēseruistī?'

lūcem: lūx *light, daylight*
perficerent: perficere *finish*
dēdicāre *dedicate*
operī: opus *work, construction*
redēmptor *contractor, builder*
flāgitābat: flāgitāre *nag at, put pressure on*
dēfessī: dēfessus *exhausted, tired out*
identidem *repeatedly*
ultimae: ultimus *last*
litterae: littera *letter*
massae: massa *block*
silēbat: silēre *be silent*
dolōre: dolor *grief*
affectae: affectus *overcome*
respice: respicere *look at, look upon*
quārē? *why?*

6

SENATVS
POPVLVSQVEROMANV
DIVOTITODIVIVESPAS
VESPASIANOAVGVST

When you have read section I of this story, answer the questions at the end of the section.

Masada

I

ex carcere obscūrō, ubi captīvī custōdiēbantur, trīstēs clāmōrēs tollēbantur. duae enim fēminae Iūdaeae, superstitēs eōrum quī contrā Rōmānōs rebellāverant, fortūnam suam lūgēbant. altera erat anus septuāgintā annōrum, altera mātrōna trīgintā annōs nāta. ūnā cum eīs in carcere erant quīnque līberī, quōrum Simōn nātū 5 maximus sōlācium mātrī et aviae ferre temptābat.

'māter, nōlī dolōrī indulgēre! decōrum est Iūdaeīs fortitūdinem in rēbus adversīs praestāre.'

māter fīlium amplexa,

'melius erat', inquit, 'cum patre vestrō perīre abhinc annōs 10 novem. cūr tum ā morte abhorruī? cūr vōs servāvī?'

Simōn, hīs verbīs commōtus, mātrem rogāvit quō modō periisset pater atque quārē rem prius nōn nārrāvisset. eam ōrāvit ut omnia explicāret. sed tantus erat dolor mātris ut prīmō nihil dīcere posset. mox, cum sē collēgisset, ad fīliōs conversa, 15

'dē morte patris vestrī', inquit, 'prius nārrāre nōlēbam nē vōs quoque perīrētis, exemplum eius imitātī. nunc tamen audeō vōbīs tōtam rem patefacere quod nōs omnēs crās moritūrī sumus.

'nōs Iūdaeī contrā Rōmānōs trēs annōs ācriter rebellāvimus. annō quārtō iste Beelzebub, Titus, urbem Ierosolymam 20 expugnāvit. numquam ego spectāculum terribilius vīdī: ubīque aedificia flammīs cōnsūmēbantur; ubīque virī, fēminae, līberī occīdēbantur; Templum ipsum ā mīlitibus dīripiēbātur; tōta urbs ēvertēbātur. in illā clāde periērunt multa mīlia Iūdaeōrum; sed circiter mīlle superstitēs, duce Eleazārō, rūpem Masadam 25 occupāvērunt. tū, Simōn, illō tempore vix quīnque annōs nātus erās.

superstitēs: superstes *survivor*
rebellāverant: rebellāre *rebel, revolt*
lūgēbant: lūgēre *lament, mourn*
altera . . . altera *one . . . the other*
. . . annōs nāta . . . *years old*
ūnā cum *together with*
nātū maximus *eldest*
aviae: avia *grandmother*
indulgēre *give way*
rēbus adversīs: rēs adversae *misfortune*
amplexa: amplexus *having embraced*
abhinc *ago*
abhorruī: abhorrēre *shrink (from)*
exemplum *example*
imitātī: imitātus *having imitated*
crās *tomorrow*
Beelzebub *Beelzebub, devil*
Ierosolymam: Ierosolyma *Jerusalem*
expugnāvit: expugnāre *storm, take by storm*
ubīque *everywhere*
circiter *about*
duce: dux *leader*
rūpem: rūpēs *rock, crag*

Coin of A.D.71 commemorating the fall of Jerusalem. To the left of the palm stands a victorious prince; to the right sits a Jewish captive.

The rock of Masada, showing the Jewish fortifications. Notice the Roman camp in the bottom right corner and some of the Roman fortifications immediately above it.

'rūpēs Masada est alta et undique praerupta, prope lacum
Asphaltītēn sita. ibi nōs, mūnītiōnibus validīs dēfēnsī, Rōmānīs diū
resistēbāmus. intereā dux hostium, Lūcius Flāvius Silva, rūpem   30
castellīs multīs circumvēnit. tum mīlitēs, iussū Silvae, ingentem
aggerem usque ad summam rūpem exstrūxērunt. deinde aggerem
ascendērunt, magnamque partem mūnītiōnum ignī dēlēvērunt.
simulatque hoc effēcērunt, Silva mīlitēs ad castra redūxit ut
proximum diem victōriamque exspectārent.'   35

undique *on all sides*
lacum Asphaltītēn: lacus Asphaltītēs *Lake Asphaltites (the Dead Sea)*
mūnītiōnibus: mūnītiō *defence, fortification*
validīs: validus *strong*
castellīs: castellum *fort*
iussū Silvae *at Silva's order*
aggerem: agger *ramp, mound of earth*
usque ad *right up to*
ignī: ignis *fire*

1 How old were the two women? How many children were with
  them in the prison? How were the children related to the two
  women?
2 How many years previously had the children's father died?
3 What two questions did Simon ask? What was his mother's
  answer to his second question?
4 What disaster had happened to the Jews in the fourth year of their
  revolt from the Romans?
5 What action was taken by a thousand Jewish survivors? Who was
  their leader?
6 Judging from lines 28–9, and the picture opposite, why do you
  think the Jews at Masada were able to hold out for so long against
  the Romans?
7 Who was the Roman general at Masada? What method did he
  use to get his men to the top of the rock? Identify it in the picture.

II

'illā nocte Eleazārus, dē rērum statū dēspērāns, Iūdaeīs cōnsilium dīrum prōposuit. '"magnō in discrīmine sumus", inquit. "nōs Iūdaeī, Deō cōnfīsī, Rōmānīs adhūc resistimus; nunc illī nōs in servitūtem trahere parant. nūlla spēs salūtis nōbīs ostenditur. nōnne melius est perīre 5 quam Rōmānīs cēdere? ego ipse mortem meā manū īnflīctam accipiō, servitūtem spernō."

'hīs verbīs Eleazārus Iūdaeīs persuāsit ut mortem sibi cōnscīscerent. tantum ardōrem in eīs excitāvit ut, simulac fīnem ōrātiōnī fēcit, ad exitium statim festīnārent. virī uxōrēs līberōsque 10 amplexī occīdērunt. cum hanc dīram et saevam rem cōnfēcissent, decem eōrum sorte ductī cēterōs interfēcērunt. tum ūnus ex illīs, sorte invicem ductus, postquam novem reliquōs mortī dedit, sē ipsum ferrō trānsfīxit.'

'quō modō nōs ipsī effūgimus?' rogāvit Simōn.   15

'ego Eleazārō pārēre nōn potuī', respondit māter. 'vōbīscum in specū latēbam.'

'ignāva!' clāmāvit Simōn. 'ego mortem haudquāquam timeō. ego, patris exemplī memor, eandem fortitūdinem praestāre volō.'

rērum statū: rērum status
  situation, state of affairs
discrīmine: discrīmen *crisis*
cōnfīsī: cōnfīsus *having trusted,*
  having put trust
servitūtem: servitūs *slavery*
īnflīctam: īnflīgere *inflict*
mortem sibi cōnscīscerent: mortem
  sibi cōnscīscere *commit suicide*
ardōrem: ardor *spirit, enthusiasm*
sorte ductī *chosen by lot*
reliquōs: reliquus *remaining*
ferrō: ferrum *sword*
specū: specus *cave*
memor *remembering, mindful of*
eandem *the same*

**Potsherd from Masada
with the name Ben Ya'ir,
or Eleazarus.**

About the language

1 In Unit I, you met sentences like these:

puer clāmōrem **audit**.   A boy hears the shout.
ancilla vīnum **fundēbat**.   A slave-girl was pouring wine.

The words in heavy print are *active* forms of the verb.

2 In Stage 29, you have met sentences like these:

clāmor ā puerō **audītur**.   The shout is heard by a boy.
vīnum ab ancillā **fundēbātur**.   Wine was being poured by a slave-girl.

The words in heavy print are *passive* forms of the verb.

3 Compare the following active and passive forms:

present tense

present active	*present passive*
portat	portātur
he carries	he is carried, *or* he is being carried
portant	portantur
they carry	they are carried, *or* they are being carried

imperfect tense

imperfect active	*imperfect passive*
portābat	portābātur
he was carrying	he was being carried
portābant	portābantur
they were carrying	they were being carried

4 Further examples of the present passive:

1 cēna nostra ā coquō nunc parātur. (Compare this with the active form: coquus cēnam nostram nunc parat.)
2 multa scelera in hāc urbe cotīdiē committuntur.
3 laudantur; dūcitur; rogātur; mittuntur.

Further examples of the imperfect passive:

4 candidātī ab amīcīs salūtābantur.
(Compare: amīcī candidātōs salūtābant.)
5 fābula ab āctōribus in theātrō agēbātur.
6 audiēbantur; laudābātur; necābantur; tenēbātur.

arcus Titī

I

postrīdiē māne ingēns Rōmānōrum multitūdō ad arcum Titī
conveniēbat. diēs fēstus ab omnibus cīvibus celebrābātur.
Imperātor Domitiānus, quod eō diē frātrī Titō arcum dēdicātūrus
erat, pompam magnificam nūntiāverat. clāmōrēs virōrum
fēminārumque undique tollēbantur. spectātōrum tanta erat 5
multitūdō ut eī quī tardius advēnērunt nūllum locum prope arcum
invenīre possent. eīs cōnsistendum erat procul ab arcū vel in forō vel
in viīs. nam iussū Imperātōris pompa tōtam per urbem dūcēbātur.
    multae sellae ā servīs prope arcum pōnēbantur. illūc multī
senātōrēs, spē favōris Domitiānī, conveniēbant. inter eōs Salvius, 10
togam splendidam gerēns, locum quaerēbat ubi cōnspicuus esset.

inter equitēs, quī post senātōrēs stābant, aderat Haterius ipse.
favōrem Imperātōris avidē spērābat, et in animō volvēbat quandō ā
Salviō praemium prōmissum acceptūrus esset.

āra ingēns, prō arcū exstrūcta, ā servīs flōribus ōrnābātur. vīgintī 15
sacerdōtēs, togās praetextās gerentēs, circum āram stābant.
haruspicēs quoque aderant quī exta victimārum īnspicerent. avium
cursus ab auguribus dīligenter notābātur.

dēdicātūrus *going to dedicate*
tardius *too late*
vel . . . vel *either . . . or*
cōnspicuus *conspicuous, easily seen*
equitēs *equites (well-to-do men
  ranking below senators)*
quandō *when*

acceptūrus *going to receive*
exta *entrails*
avium: avis *bird*
cursus *flight*
auguribus: augur *augur*
notābātur: notāre *note, observe*

II

intereā pompa lentē per Viam Sacram dūcēbātur. prīmā in parte
incēdēbant tubicinēs tubās īnflantēs. post eōs vēnērunt iuvenēs quī
trīgintā taurōs corōnīs ōrnātōs ad sacrificium dūcēbant. tum multī
servī, quī gāzam Iūdaeōrum portābant, prīmam pompae partem
claudēbant. huius gāzae pars pretiōsissima erat mēnsa sacra, tubae, 5
candēlābrum, quae omnia aurea erant.

septem captīvī Iūdaeī, quī mediā in pompā incēdēbant, ā
spectātōribus vehementer dērīdēbantur. quīnque puerī, serēnō

gāzam: gāza *treasure*　　　　　　claudēbant: claudere *conclude, complete*

vultū incēdentēs, clāmōrēs et contumēliās neglegēbant, sed duae
fēminae plūrimīs lacrimīs spectātōrēs ōrābant ut līberīs parcerent. 10
post captīvōs vēnit Domitiānus ipse, currū magnificō vectus. quia
Pontifex Maximus erat, togam praetextam gerēbat. post
Imperātōrem ambō ībant cōnsulēs, quōrum alter erat L. Flāvius
Silva. cōnsulēs et magistrātūs nōbilissimī effigiem Titī in umerīs
portābant. ā mīlitibus pompa claudēbātur. 15
  ad arcum pompa pervēnit. Domitiānus, ē currū ēgressus ut
sacrificium faceret, senātōrēs magistrātūsque salūtāvit. tum oculōs
in arcum ipsum convertit. admīrātiōne affectus, Imperātor Salvium
ad sē arcessītum maximē laudāvit. eī imperāvit ut Hateriō grātiās
ageret. inde ad āram prōgressus, cultrum cēpit quō victimam 20
sacrificāret. servus eī iugulum taurī obtulit. deinde Domitiānus,
victimam sacrificāns, frātrī Titō precēs adhibuit:
  'tibi, dīve Tite, haec victima nunc sacrificātur; tibi hic arcus
dēdicātur; tibi precēs populī Rōmānī adhibentur.'
  subitō, dum Rōmānī oculōs in sacrificium intentē dēfīgunt, 25
Simōn occāsiōnem nactus prōsiluit. mediōs in sacerdōtēs irrūpit;
cultrum rapuit. omnēs spectātōrēs immōtī stābant, audāciā eius
attonitī. Domitiānus, pavōre commōtus, pedem rettulit. nōn
Imperātōrem tamen, sed mātrem, aviam, frātrēs Simōn petīvit.
cultrum in manū tenēns clāmāvit, 30
  'nōs, quī superstitēs Iūdaeōrum rebellantium sumus, Rōmānīs
servīre nōlumus. mortem obīre mālumus.'
  haec locūtus, facinus dīrum commīsit. mātrem et aviam
amplexus cultrō statim occīdit. tum frātrēs, haudquāquam
resistentēs, eōdem modō interfēcit. postrēmō magnā vōce populum 35
Rōmānum dētestātus sē ipsum cultrō trānsfīxit.

vultū: vultus *expression, face*   inde *then*
currū: currus *chariot*   cultrum: culter *knife*
vectus: vehere *carry*   dīve: dīvus *god*
quia *because*   dum *while*
Pontifex Maximus *Chief Priest*   dēfīgunt: dēfīgere *fix*
cōnsulēs: cōnsul *consul (senior magistrate)*   nactus *having seized*
magistrātūs: magistrātus *magistrate*   pedem rettulit: pedem referre *step back*
    (*elected official of Roman government*)   mālumus: mālle *prefer*
admīrātiōne: admīrātiō *admiration*   eōdem modō *in the same way*

About the language

1 In Stage 26, you met purpose clauses used with 'ut':

senex īnsidiās īnstrūxit ut fūrēs caperet.
The old man set a trap in order that he might catch the thieves.
  or, in more natural English:
The old man set a trap to catch the thieves.

2 In Stage 29, you have met purpose clauses used with part of the relative pronoun 'quī':

fēmina servum mīsit quī cibum emeret.
The woman sent a slave who was to buy food.
  or, in more natural English:
The woman sent a slave to buy food.

You have also met purpose clauses used with 'ubi':

locum quaerēbāmus ubi stārēmus.
We were looking for a place where we might stand.
  or, in more natural English:
We were looking for a place to stand.

3 Further examples:

1 sacerdōs haruspicem arcessīvit quī exta īnspiceret.
2 senātor gemmam pretiōsam quaerēbat quam uxōrī daret.
3 Haterius quīnque fabrōs ēlēgit quī figūrās in arcū sculperent.
4 domum emere volēbam ubi fīlius meus habitāret.

Practising the language

1   Study the way in which the following verbs are formed, and give
    the meaning of the untranslated ones:

currere	dēcurrere	excurrere	recurrere
run	run down	run out	run back
iacere	dēicere	ēicere	reicere
throw			throw back
trahere	dētrahere	extrahere	retrahere
pull, drag	pull down		
salīre	dēsilīre	exsilīre	resilīre
jump		jump out	
cadere	dēcidere	excidere	recidere
fall		fall out	

The verbs in the second, third and fourth columns are known as
compound verbs.

Give the meaning of the following compound verbs:

exīre, ēmittere, expellere, ērumpere, effundere;
dēmittere, dēpōnere, dēspicere;
redūcere, remittere, redīre, respicere, repōnere, referre,
revenīre, recipere, revocāre.

2 Complete each sentence with the right form of the imperfect subjunctive, using the verb in brackets, then translate.

For example: equitēs īnsidiās parāvērunt ut ducem hostium
. . . . . . (capere)
Answer: equitēs īnsidiās parāvērunt ut ducem hostium
caperent.
The cavalry prepared a trap in order to catch the leader of the enemy.

The forms of the imperfect subjunctive are given on page 142 in the Language Information section.

1 fabrī strēnuē labōrāvērunt ut arcum . . . . . . (perficere)
2 Domitiānus ad āram prōcessit ut victimam . . . . . .
(sacrificāre)
3 ad forum contendēbāmus ut pompam . . . . . . (spectāre)
4 barbarī facēs in manibus tenēbant ut templum . . . . . .
(incendere)
5 extrā carcerem stābam ut captīvōs . . . . . . (custōdīre)

3 Complete each sentence with the most suitable participle from the lists below, using the correct form, and then translate. Do not use any participle more than once.

dūcēns	labōrāns	sedēns	incēdēns	clāmāns
dūcentem	labōrantem	sedentem	incēdentem	clāmantem
dūcentēs	labōrantēs	sedentēs	incēdentēs	clāmantēs

1 videō Salvium prope arcum . . . . . .
2 fabrī, in Viā Sacrā . . . . ., valdē dēfessī erant.
3 nōnne audīs puerōs . . . . .?
4 iuvenis, victimam . . . . ., ad āram prōcessit.
5 spectātōrēs captīvōs, per viās . . . . ., dērīdēbant.

4 Translate each English sentence into Latin by selecting correctly from the list of Latin words.

1 The citizens, having been delighted by the show, applauded.

cīvis   spectāculum   dēlectātus   plaudunt
cīvēs   spectāculō   dēlectātī   plausērunt

2 I recognised the slave-girl who was pouring the wine.

ancilla   quī   vīnum   fundēbat   agnōvī
ancillam   quae   vīnō   fundēbant   agnōvit

3 Having returned to the bank of the river, the soldiers halted.

ad rīpam   flūmine   regressī   mīlitēs   cōnstitērunt
ad rīpās   flūminis   regressōs   mīlitum   cōnstiterant

4 The woman, sitting in prison, told a sad story.

fēmina   in carcerem   sedēns   fābulam   trīstis   nārrat
fēminae   in carcere   sedentem   fābulae   trīstem   nārrāvit

5 We saw the altar, decorated with flowers.

āram   flōrī   ōrnāta   vīdī
ārās   flōribus   ōrnātam   vīdimus

6 They killed the sleeping prisoners with swords.

captīvī   dormientem   gladiōs   occīdērunt
captīvōs   dormientēs   gladiīs   occīdit

The Roman forum

The forum of Rome (forum Rōmānum) was not only the social and commercial centre of the city; it was the centre of the whole empire. To symbolise this, the Emperor Augustus placed a golden milestone (mīliārium aureum) in the forum to mark the starting-point of the roads that radiated from the city to all the corners of the empire.

The ordinary people of Rome came in great numbers to the forum, sometimes to visit its temples and public buildings, sometimes to listen to speeches or watch a procession, and sometimes just to meet their friends and stroll idly about, pausing at

The forum.

times to gossip, listen to an argument, or bargain with a passing street-trader.

In the great halls (basilicae), lawyers pleaded their cases in front of large and often noisy audiences, and merchants and bankers negotiated their business deals. Senators made their way to the senate-house (cūria) to conduct the affairs of government under the leadership of the emperor. Sometimes a funeral procession wound its way through the forum, accompanied by noisy lamentations and

21

loud music; sometimes the crowd was forced to make way for a wealthy noble, who was carried through the forum in a sedan-chair by his slaves and escorted by a long line of citizens.

The forum lay on low ground between two of Rome's hills, the Capitol and the Palatine. On the Capitol at the western end of the forum stood the temple of Jupiter Optimus Maximus, the centre of the Roman state religion. This was where the emperor came to pray for the continued safety of the Roman people; and this was where the consuls took their solemn vows on January 1st each year at the beginning of their consulship. On the Palatine stood the emperor's residence. In the time of Augustus, this had been a small and simple house; later emperors built palaces of steadily increasing splendour.

Near the foot of the Capitol stood the Rostra, a platform from which public speeches were made to the people. It took its name from the 'rōstra' (ships' prows, which had been captured in a sea battle early in Rome's history) which were used to decorate it. One of the most famous speeches made from the Rostra was Mark Antony's speech over the body of Julius Caesar in 44 B.C. The listening crowds were so carried away by Antony's words and so angry at Caesar's murder that they rioted, seized the body, and burned it in the forum. A temple was later built in Caesar's memory at the eastern end of the forum, on the spot where his body had been burned.

Not far from the Rostra was the prison. Prisoners of war, like the seven Jews in the stories of this Stage, were held in the prison before being led in a triumphal procession through the streets of Rome. Afterwards they were taken back to the prison and killed.

Near the temple of Julius Caesar was a small round building with a cone-shaped roof. This was the temple of Vesta, where the Vestal Virgins tended the sacred flame of the city so that it would burn for ever.

Through the forum ran the Sacred Way (Via Sacra), which provided an avenue for religious or triumphal processions. When the Romans celebrated a victory in war, the triumphal procession passed through the city and ended by travelling along the Sacred Way towards the temple of Jupiter on the Capitol, where the victorious general gave thanks. The story on pp. 14–16 describes a rather similar occasion: the dedication of the arch of Titus by the Emperor Domitian in A.D. 81. On this occasion, the procession would have followed the Sacred Way eastwards out of the forum, up a gentle slope to the site of the arch itself. The arch commemorated the victory of Domitian's brother Titus over the Jewish people. The Jews' last stand at Masada, their fortress near the Dead Sea, is described in the story on pp. 8–12.

The forum Romanum was not the only forum in the city. By the time of the events of this Stage, two other forums had been built by Julius Caesar and Augustus; later, two more were added by the Emperors Nerva and Trajan. The most splendid of these was Trajan's forum, which contained the famous column commemorating Trajan's victories over the Dacians. But none of these other forums replaced the forum Romanum as the political, religious and social heart of the city. If one Roman said to another, 'I'll meet you in the forum', he meant the forum Romanum.

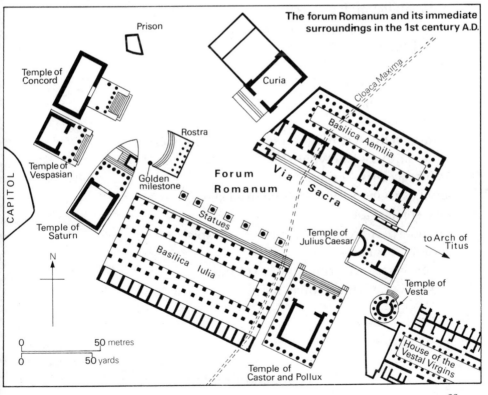

The forum Romanum and its immediate surroundings in the 1st century A.D.

Words and phrases checklist

aliī . . . aliī – some . . . others
aliquandō – sometimes
amplexus, amplexa, amplexum – having embraced
audācia, audāciae – boldness, audacity
carmen, carminis – song
circumveniō, circumvenīre, circumvēnī, circumventus – surround
corōna, corōnae – garland, wreath
cursus, cursūs – course, flight
dēfessus, dēfessa, dēfessum – exhausted, tired out
dolor, dolōris – grief, pain
ferrum, ferrī – iron, sword
incēdō, incēdere, incessī – march, stride
līberī, līberōrum – children
lūx, lūcis – light, daylight
mālō, mālle, māluī – prefer
obscūrus, obscūra, obscūrum – dark, gloomy
ōdī – I hate
perficiō, perficere, perfēcī, perfectus – finish
populus, populī – people
prius – earlier
quiēs, quiētis – rest
redūcō, redūcere, redūxī, reductus – lead back
salūs, salūtis – safety, health
scelus, sceleris – crime
serviō, servīre, servīvī – serve (as a slave)
sors, sortis – lot
spernō, spernere, sprēvī, sprētus – despise, reject
undique – on all sides
vester, vestra, vestrum – your (plural)
vīvus, vīva, vīvum – alive, living

Haterius

Haterius: quam fēlīx sum!
heri arcus meus ab Imperātōre dēdicātus est.
heri praemium ingēns mihi ā Salviō prōmissum est.
hodiē praemium exspectō . . .

Haterius: anxius sum.
arcus meus nūper ab Imperātōre laudātus est.
nūllum tamen praemium adhūc mihi ā Salviō missum est.
num ego ā Salviō dēceptus sum?
minimē! Salvius vir probus est . . .

When you have read this story, answer the questions at the end.

dignitās

cīvēs Rōmānī, postquam arcus ab Imperātōre dēdicātus est,
quattuor diēs fēstōs celebrāvērunt. templa vīsitābant ut dīs grātiās
agerent; Circum Maximum cotīdiē complēbant ut lūdōs magnificōs
ā cōnsulibus ēditōs spectārent; ad arcum ipsum conveniēbant ut
figūrās in eō sculptās īnspicerent. plūrimī clientēs domum Salviī 5
veniēbant quī grātulātiōnēs eī facerent. Salvius ipse summō gaudiō
affectus est quod Imperātor arcum Hateriī valdē laudāverat.
    apud Haterium tamen nūllae grātulantium vōcēs audītae sunt.
neque clientēs neque amīcī ab eō admissī sunt. Haterius, īrā
commōtus, sōlus domī manēbat. adeō saeviēbat ut dormīre nōn 10

dīs = deīs: deus *god*
Circum Maximum: Circus Maximus
   the Circus Maximus (stadium
   for chariot-racing)
ēditōs: ēdere *put on, present*

clientēs: cliēns *client*
grātulātiōnēs: grātulātiō *congratulation*
gaudiō: gaudium *joy*
grātulantium: grātulāns *congratulating*

**Busts from the reliefs on the tomb of the Haterii, possibly Haterius and
Vitellia.**

27

posset. quattuor diēs noctēsque vigilābat. quīntō diē uxor, Vitellia nōmine, quae nesciēbat quārē Haterius adeō īrātus esset, eum mollīre temptābat. ingressa hortum, ubi Haterius hūc illūc ambulābat, eum anxia interrogāvit.

Vitellia: cūr tam vehementer saevīs, mī Haterī? et amīcōs et 15 clientēs, quī vēnērunt ut tē salūtārent, domō abēgistī. neque ūnum verbum mihi hōs quattuor diēs dīxistī. sine dubiō, ut istum arcum cōnficerēs, nimis labōrāvistī, neglegēns valētūdinis tuae. nōnne melius est tibi ad vīllam rūsticam mēcum abīre? nam rūrī, cūrās oblītus, 20 quiēscere potes.

Haterius: quō modō ego, tantam iniūriam passus, quiēscere possum?

Vitellia: verba tua nōn intellegō. quis tibi iniūriam intulit?

Haterius: ego ā Salviō, quī mihi favēre solēbat, omnīnō dēceptus 25 sum. prō omnibus meīs labōribus ingēns praemium mihi ā Salviō prōmissum est. nūllum praemium tamen, nē grātiās quidem, accēpī.

Vitellia: contentus estō, mī Haterī! redēmptor nōtissimus es, cuius arcus ab Imperātōre ipsō nūper laudātus est. multa 30 aedificia pūblica exstrūxistī, unde magnās dīvitiās comparāvistī.

Haterius: dīvitiās floccī nōn faciō. in hāc urbe sunt plūrimī redēmptōrēs quī opēs maximās comparāvērunt. mihi autem nōn dīvitiae sed dignitās est cūrae. 35

Vitellia: dignitās tua amplissima est. nam nōn modo dītissimus es sed etiam uxōrem nōbilissimā gente nātam habēs. Rūfilla, soror mea, uxor est Salviī quī tibi semper fāvit et saepe tē Imperātōrī commendāvit. quid aliud ā Salviō accipere cupis? 40

Haterius: volō ad summōs honōrēs pervenīre, sīcut illī Hateriī quī abhinc multōs annōs cōnsulēs factī sunt. praesertim sacerdōs esse cupiō; multī enim virī, sacerdōtēs ab Imperātōre creātī, posteā ad cōnsulātum pervēnērunt. sed Salvius, quamquam sacerdōtium mihi identidem 45 prōmīsit, fidem nōn servāvit.

Vitellia: nōlī dēspērāre, mī Haterī! melius est tibi ad Salvium īre
blandīsque verbīs ab eō hunc honōrem repetere.
Haterius: mihi, quī redēmptor optimus sum, nōn decōrum est
honōrēs ita quaerere.   50
Vitellia: cōnsilium optimum habeō. invītā Salvium ad āream
tuam! ostentā eī polyspaston tuum! nihil maius nec
mīrābilius umquam anteā factum est. deinde Salvium
admīrātiōne affectum rogā dē sacerdōtiō.

vigilābat: vigilāre *stay awake*
quīntō: quīntus *fifth*
hūc illūc *here and there, up and down*
abēgistī: abigere *drive away*
valētūdinis: valētūdō *health*
rūrī *in the country*
oblītus *having forgotten*
nē . . . quidem *not even*
estō! *be!*
pūblica: pūblicus *public*
dīvitiās: dīvitiae *riches*
est cūrae *is a matter of concern*

amplissima: amplissimus *very great*
dītissimus: dīves *rich*
commendāvit: commendāre *recommend*
cōnsulātum: cōnsulātus *consulship*
  (rank of consul)
sacerdōtium *priesthood*
fidem . . . servāvit: fidem servāre *keep*
  a promise, keep faith
āream: ārea *building-site*
ostentā: ostentāre *show off, display*
nec *nor*

1 How long was the holiday which followed the dedication of the
arch? During this holiday, what happened (*a*) in the temples, (*b*)
at the Circus Maximus, (*c*) at the arch itself?
2 Why did Salvius' clients come to his house? What happened to
the clients of Haterius?
3 What does Vitellia at first think is the matter with Haterius?
What action does she suggest?
4 In what way does Haterius consider he has been badly treated?
5 Explain Haterius' reason for saying 'dīvitiās floccī nōn faciō' (line
33).
6 What honour does Haterius want to receive in the near future?
What does he hope this will lead to?
7 Why does Haterius reject the advice given by Vitellia in lines
47–8? Explain what Haterius means by 'ita' (line 50).
8 What suggestion does Vitellia make in lines 51–2? How does she
think this will help Haterius to get what he wants?

About the language

1   In this Stage, you have met the *perfect passive*. Compare it with the perfect active:

perfect active

senex fūrem **accūsāvit**.	The old man has accused the thief.
	or, The old man accused the thief.
Rōmānī hostēs **superāvērunt**.	The Romans have overcome the enemy.
	or, The Romans overcame the enemy.

perfect passive

fūr ā sene **accūsātus est**.	The thief has been accused by the old man.
	or, The thief was accused by the old man.
hostēs ā Rōmānīs **superātī sunt**.	The enemy have been overcome by the Romans.
	or, The enemy were overcome by the Romans.

2   The forms of the perfect passive are as follows:

portātus sum	I have been carried, *or* I was carried
portātus es	you (s.) have been carried, *or* you were carried
portātus est	he has been carried, *or* he was carried
portātī sumus	we have been carried, *or* we were carried
portātī estis	you (pl.) have been carried, *or* you were carried
portātī sunt	they have been carried, *or* they were carried

3   Notice that each form of the perfect passive is made up of two words:

1   a perfect passive participle (e.g. 'portātus') in either a singular or a plural form,
2   a form of the present tense of 'sum'.

4 Further examples:

1 arcus ab Imperātōre dēdicātus est.
   (Compare: Imperātor arcum dēdicāvit.)
2 multī nūntiī ad urbem missī sunt.
3 dux hostium ā mīlitibus captus est.
4 audītus est; invītātī sunt; dēceptī sumus; laudātus es.

---

polyspaston

---

postrīdiē Haterius Salvium ad āream suam dūxit ut polyspaston eī
ostentāret. ibi sedēbat ōtiōsus Glitus magister fabrōrum. quī cum
dominum   appropinquantem   cōnspexisset,   celeriter   surrēxit
fabrōsque dīligentius labōrāre iussit.

tōta ārea strepitū labōrantium plēna erat. columnae ex marmore 5
pretiōsissimō secābantur; laterēs in āream portābantur; ingentēs
marmoris massae in plaustra pōnēbantur. Haterius, cum fabrōs
labōre occupātōs vīdisset, Salvium ad aliam āreae partem dūxit. ibi
stābat ingēns polyspaston quod ā fabrīs parātum erat. in tignō
polyspastī sēdēs fīxa erat. tum Haterius ad Salvium versus, 10
   'mī Salvī', inquit, 'nōnne mīrābile est hoc polyspaston? fabrī meī
id exstrūxērunt ut marmor ad summum arcum tollerent. nunc
autem tibi tālem urbis prōspectum praestāre volō quālem paucī
umquam vīdērunt. placetne tibi?'
   Salvius, ubi sēdem in tignō fīxam vīdit, palluit. sed, quod fabrī 15
oculōs in eum dēfīxōs habēbant, timōrem dissimulāns in sēdem

laterēs: later *brick*
tignō: tignum *beam*
sēdēs *seat*
fīxa erat: fīgere *fix, fasten*
tālem . . . quālem *such . . . as*
prōspectum: prōspectus *view*
timōrem: timor *fear*
dissimulāns: dissimulāre *conceal, hide*

cōnsēdit. iuxtā eum Haterius quoque cōnsēdit. tum fabrīs imperāvit
ut fūnēs, quī ad tignum adligātī erant, summīs vīribus traherent.
deinde tignum lentē ad caelum tollēbātur. Salvius pavōre paene
cōnfectus clausīs oculīs ad sēdem haerēbat. ubi tandem oculōs 20
aperuit, spectāculō attonitus,
   'dī immortālēs!' inquit. 'tōtam urbem vidēre possum. ecce
templum Iovis! ecce flūmen! ecce amphitheātrum Flāvium et arcus
novus! quam in sōle fulget! Imperātor, simulatque illum arcum
vīdit, summā admīrātiōne affectus est. mihi imperāvit ut grātiās 25
suās tibi agerem.'
   cui respondit Haterius,
   'maximē gaudeō quod opus meum ab Imperātōre laudātum est.
sed praemium illud quod tū mihi prōmīsistī nōndum accēpī.'
   Salvius tamen vōce blandā,   30
   'dē sacerdōtiō tuō', inquit, 'Imperātōrem iam saepe cōnsuluī, et
respōnsum eius etiam nunc exspectō. aliquid tamen tibi intereā
offerre possum. agellum quendam possideō, quī prope sepulcra
Metellōrum et Scīpiōnum situs est. tūne hunc agellum emere velīs?'
   quae cum audīvisset, Haterius tantō gaudiō affectus est ut dē 35
tignō paene dēcideret.
   'ita vērō', inquit, 'in illō agellō, prope sepulcra gentium
nōbilissimārum, ego quoque sepulcrum splendidum mihi meīsque
exstruere velim, figūrīs operum meōrum ōrnātum; ita enim nōmen
factaque mea posterīs trādere possum. prō agellō tuō igitur 40
sēstertium vīciēns tibi offerō.'
   Salvius sibi rīsit; agellus enim eī grātīs ab Imperātōre datus erat.
   'agellus multō plūris est', inquit, 'sed quod patrōnus sum tuus tibi
faveō. mē iuvat igitur sēstertium tantum trīciēns ā tē accipere.
placetne tibi?'   45
   Haterius libenter cōnsēnsit. tum fabrīs imperāvit ut tignum lentē
dēmitterent. itaque ambō humum rediērunt, alter spē
immortālitātis ēlātus, alter praesentī pecūniā contentus.

iuxtā *next to*
fūnēs: fūnis *rope*
adligātī erant: adligāre *tie*
vīribus: vīrēs *strength*
Iovis: Iuppiter *Jupiter (god of the sky,*
  greatest of Roman gods)
amphitheātrum Flāvium *Flavian*
  amphitheatre (now known as Colosseum)
nōndum *not yet*
blandā: blandus *flattering, charming*
agellum: agellus *small plot of land*
quendam: quīdam *one, a certain*
sepulcra: sepulcrum *tomb*
Metellōrum: Metellī *the Metelli*
  (famous Roman family)
Scīpiōnum: Scīpiōnēs *the Scipiones*
  (famous Roman family)
meīs: meī *my family*
facta: factum *deed, achievement*
posterīs: posterī *future generations,*
  posterity
sēstertium vīciēns *two million sesterces*
multō plūris est *is worth much more*
mē iuvat *it pleases me*
sēstertium . . . trīciēns *three million*
  sesterces
humum *to the ground*
immortālitātis: immortālitās
  immortality
ēlātus *thrilled, excited*
praesentī: praesēns *present, ready*

**Crane from the reliefs on the tomb
of the Haterii.**

About the language

1 You have now met the *pluperfect passive*. Compare it with the pluperfect active:

pluperfect active
servus dominum **vulnerāverat**. A slave had wounded the master.

pluperfect passive
dominus ā servō **vulnerātus erat**. The master had been wounded by a slave.

2 The forms of the pluperfect passive are as follows:

portātus eram	I had been carried
portātus erās	you (s.) had been carried
portātus erat	he had been carried
portātī erāmus	we had been carried
portātī erātis	you (pl.) had been carried
portātī erant	they had been carried

Each form of the pluperfect passive is made up of a perfect passive participle (e.g. 'portātus') and a form of the imperfect tense of 'sum' (e.g. 'erat').

3 Further examples:

1 Simōn ā mātre servātus erat.
   (Compare: māter Simōnem servāverat.)
2 custōdēs prope arcum positī erant.
3 fabrī dīligenter labōrāre iussī erant.
4 Haterius ā Salviō dēceptus erat.
5 pūnītī erant; missus erat; audītus eram.

Practising the language

1 Study the form and meaning of the following adjectives and nouns, and give the meaning of the untranslated words:

benignus	kind	benignitās	kindness
īnfirmus	weak	īnfirmitās	weakness
suāvis	sweet	suāvitās	
probus	honest	probitās	
līber		lībertās	freedom
avidus		aviditās	eagerness, greed
immortālis		immortālitās	
gravis	heavy, serious	gravitās	
sevērus		sevēritās	
celer		celeritās	speed
līberālis		līberālitās	generosity

Give the meaning of the following nouns:

crūdēlitās, tranquillitās, calliditās, ūtilitās, paupertās, caecitās, fēlīcitās

2 Translate each sentence; then, with the help of the table of nouns on pages 128 and 129 in the Language Information section, change the words in heavy print from singular to plural, and translate again.

1 mīles perfidus **amīcum** dēseruit.
2 dux virtūtem **legiōnis** laudāvit.
3 Imperātor multōs honōrēs **lībertō** dedit.
4 iūdex epistulam **testī** trādidit.
5 hostēs in **silvā** latēbant.
6 puella, **flōre** dēlectāta, suāviter rīsit.
7 barbarī **vīllam agricolae** incendērunt.
8 rēx pecūniam **mātrī puerī** reddidit.

3 Complete each sentence with the right word and then translate.

1 mercātor, ē carcere . . . . ., dīs grātiās ēgit. (līberātus, līberātī)
2 māter, verbīs Eleazārī . . . . ., cum līberīs in specum fūgit. (territus, territa)
3 Salvius epistulam, ab Imperātōre . . . . ., legēbat. (scrīpta, scrīptam)
4 nāvēs, tempestāte paene . . . . ., tandem ad portum revēnērunt. (dēlētus, dēlēta, dēlētae)
5 centuriō septem mīlitēs, gladiīs . . . . ., sēcum dūxit. (armātī, armātōs, armātīs)

4 Translate each pair of sentences, then link them together, using 'cum' and the pluperfect subjunctive, and translate again.

For example: hospitēs advēnērunt. coquus cēnam intulit.
This becomes: cum hospitēs advēnissent, coquus cēnam intulit.
When the guests had arrived, the cook brought the dinner in.

The forms of the pluperfect subjunctive are given on page 142 in the Language Information section.

1 barbarī fūgērunt. mīlitēs ad castra revēnērunt.
2 servus iānuam aperuit. senex intrāvit.
3 Imperātor arcum dēdicāvit. senātōrēs populusque plausērunt.
4 fabrī polyspaston parāvērunt. Haterius Salvium ad āream dūxit.
5 rem perfēcimus. domum rediimus.

Buildings from the reliefs on the tomb of the Haterii. On the left the Colosseum, in the centre a triumphal arch (shown sideways), on the right the arch of Titus.

Roman builders

The various carvings on the family tomb of the Haterii, especially the crane, suggest that at least one member of the family was a prosperous building contractor. His personal names are unknown but in the stories we have called him Quintus Haterius Latronianus. One of his contracts was for a magnificent arch to commemorate the popular Emperor Titus who died after only a short reign (A.D. 79– 81). In Stage 29, Haterius is imagined as anxiously trying to complete it during the night before its dedication by the new emperor, Domitian, and in this Stage he is seeking his reward.

Helped by an architect who provided the design and technical advice Haterius would have employed sub-contractors to supply the materials and engage the workmen. Most of these were slaves and poor free men working as unskilled, occasional labour, but there were also craftsmen such as carpenters and stonemasons. It

was the job of the carpenters to put up a timber framework to give shape and temporary support to the arches as they were being built (see diagram above). They also erected the scaffolding and made the timber moulds for shaping concrete. The masons were responsible for the quarrying of the stone and its transport, often by barge up the river Tiber, to the building-site in the city before carving the elaborate decoration and preparing the blocks to be lifted into position. The richly carved panels on Titus' arch showed the triumphal procession with prisoners and treasure captured at the sack of Jerusalem in A.D. 70.

Many of our modern handtools have been inherited almost unchanged from those used by Roman craftsmen (for instance, mallets, chisels, crowbars, trowels, saws and planes), but with the important difference that the Romans did not have the small electric motor that makes the modern power tool so much quicker and less laborious to use.

The blocks of dressed stone were lifted by man-powered cranes. The picture of Haterius' crane on page 33 shows it from the side and therefore not all the details of its design are visible. It consisted of two wooden uprights, forming the jib, fastened together at the top and splayed apart at the feet. The hoisting rope ran round two pulleys, one at the top of the jib and one at the point where the load was fastened to the rope. After passing round the pulleys the rope led down to a winding drum, which was turned by a treadmill fixed to the side of the crane and operated by two or three men inside. Smaller cranes had, instead of the treadmill, a capstan with projecting spokes to be turned by hand. This arrangement of pulleys and ropes multiplied the force exerted by human muscles so that a small crew could raise loads weighing up to eight or nine tonnes. To prevent the crane from toppling over, stayropes were stretched out from the jib, also with the help of pulleys, and firmly anchored to the ground. These machines were certainly cumbersome, slow and liable to accidents, but they worked.

Another aid to building was good quality cement. The main ingredients of this versatile and easily produced material were (1) lime mortar, made by heating pieces of limestone to a high temperature and then crushing them to a powder, (2) fine sand, (3) clay. These were combined with water to make a smooth paste. In this form the cement was an excellent adhesive which could be spread in a thin layer between bricks or stones, as we do today, and when dry it held them firmly together.

The Romans also mixed cement with rubble, such as stone chippings, broken bricks and pieces of tile, to form the inner core of a wall, sandwiched between the two faces. The advantage of this was that the more expensive material, good quality stone or brick, could be reserved for the outer faces; these were often then covered with plaster and painted in bright colours. Marble too, in thinly cut plates, was used as a facing material where cost was no object.

Another more novel use of concrete, that is cement mixed with rubble, was as a substitute for stone in the building of arches and vaulted ceilings. For the Romans found that concrete, when shaped into arches, was strong enough to span large spaces without any additional support from pillars, and that it could carry the weight of a heavy superstructure. The Romans were not the first people to make concrete but they improved its quality and applied it on a grand, revolutionary scale. They used it, for instance, on the

Interior of the dome of the Pantheon.

aqueducts that supplied Rome with millions of gallons of fresh water daily, on the Pantheon, a temple whose domed concrete and brick roof (still in good condition today) has a span of 43 metres (140 feet) and rises to the same height above the floor. They also used it on the huge Flavian amphitheatre (known from medieval times as the Colosseum), which could hold up to 50,000 spectators, and is another of Haterius' surviving buildings (see p. 102).

Not all buildings, of course, were constructed so sturdily. The inhabitants of Rome in the first century A.D. were housed in a vast number of dwellings, many of them blocks of flats (īnsulae) which were built much more cheaply, mainly of brick and timber. They had a reputation for being rickety and liable to catch fire. To reduce the danger the Emperor Augustus fixed a limit of 21 metres (70 feet) in height for these insulae and organised fire brigades.

Nevertheless, serious fires did break out from time to time. One occurred in A.D. 80 and when Domitian became emperor in the following year he continued the programme of repair that Titus had begun. He restored the spectacular temple of Jupiter Optimus˙ Maximus on the Capitol which had been badly burned in the fire. He built more temples, a stadium, a concert hall and even an artificial lake for sea fights, all no doubt to enhance the influence and majesty of the emperor.

The boast of Augustus, 'urbem latericiam accepi, marmoream reliqui' – 'I found Rome built of brick and left it made of marble', was certainly an exaggeration. For the spaces between the marble-faced public libraries, baths and temples were crammed with the homes of ordinary people. Many builders must have spent most of their time working on these dwellings, described by the poet Juvenal as 'propped up with sticks'. But given the opportunity of a large contract and a technical challenge, Roman builders made adventurous use of concrete, cranes and arches; and Domitian, who was determined to add to the splendours of his capital city, kept architects and builders very busy throughout most of his reign.

Words and phrases checklist

adhūc – up till now
afficiō, afficere, affēcī, affectus – affect, overcome
ambō, ambae, ambō – both
cōnsulō, cōnsulere, cōnsuluī, cōnsultus – consult
creō, creāre, creāvī, creātus – make, create
dēmittō, dēmittere, dēmīsī, dēmissus – let down, lower
dīves, *gen.* dīvitis – rich
dīvitiae, dīvitiārum – riches
dubium, dubiī – doubt
exstruō, exstruere, exstrūxī, exstrūctus – build
fēstus, fēsta, fēstum – festival, holiday
iniūria, iniūriae – injustice, injury
lūdus, lūdī – game
magister, magistrī – master, foreman
nātus, nāta, nātum – born
nimis – too
omnīnō – completely
opus, operis – work, construction
pallēscō, pallēscere, palluī – grow pale
pavor, pavōris – panic, terror
praestō, praestāre, praestitī – show, display
praetereā – besides
quārē? – why?
sēdēs, sēdis – seat
sepulcrum, sepulcrī – tomb
sōl, sōlis – sun
′soror, sorōris – sister
strepitus, strepitūs – noise, din
tempestās, tempestātis – storm
timor, timōris – fear

in urbe

diēs illūcēscēbat.

diē illūcēscente, multī saccāriī in rīpā flūminis labōrābant.

saccāriīs labōrantibus, advēnit nāvis. nautae nāvem dēligāvērunt.

nāve dēligātā, saccāriī frūmentum expōnere coepērunt.

frūmentō expositō, magister
nāvis pecūniam saccāriīs
distribuit.

pecūniā distribūtā, saccāriī ad
tabernam proximam
festīnāvērunt.

tandem sōl occidere coepit.

sōle occidente, saccāriī ā tabernā
ēbriī discessērunt, omnī pecūniā
cōnsūmptā.

adventus

diē illūcēscente, ingēns Rōmānōrum multitūdō viās urbis
complēbat. pauperēs ex īnsulīs exībant ut aquam ē fontibus pūblicīs
traherent. senātōrēs ad forum lectīcīs vehēbantur. in rīpīs flūminis
Tiberis, ubi multa horrea sita erant, frūmentum ē nāvibus ā
saccāriīs expōnēbātur. servī, quī ā vēnālīciīs ex Āfricā importātī 5
erant, ē nāvibus dūcēbantur, catēnīs gravibus vīnctī.

ex ūnā nāvium, quae modo ā Graeciā advēnerat, puella
pulcherrima exiit. epistulam ad Haterium scrīptam manū tenēbat.
sarcinae eius ā servō portābantur, virō quadrāgintā annōrum. tot
tantaeque erant sarcinae ut servus eās ferre vix posset. 10

sōle ortō, puella ad Subūram advēnit. multitūdine
clāmōribusque hominum valdē obstupefacta est. tanta erat
multitūdō ut puella cum summā difficultāte prōcēderet. mendīcī,
quī ad compita sedēbant, manūs ad praetereuntēs porrigēbant.
ubīque sonitus labōrantium audiēbātur: ā crepidāriīs calceī 15
reficiēbantur; ā ferrāriīs gladiī excūdēbantur; ā fabrīs tigna
secābantur. fabrī, puellā vīsā, clāmāre coepērunt; puellam verbīs
procācibus appellāvērunt. quae tamen, clāmōribus fabrōrum
neglēctīs, vultū serēnō celeriter praeteriit. servum iussit festīnāre nē
domum Hateriī tardius pervenīrent. 20

eōdem tempore multī clientēs per viās contendēbant ut patrōnōs
salūtārent. aliī, scissīs togīs ruptīsque calceīs, per lutum lentē ībant.
eīs difficile erat festīnāre quod lutum erat altum, viae angustae,
multitūdō dēnsa. aliī, quī nōbilī gente nātī sunt, celeriter
prōcēdēbant quod servī multitūdinem fūstibus dēmovēbant. 25
clientēs, quī sīcut unda per viās ruēbant, puellae prōcēdentī
obstābant.

illūcēscente: illūcēscere *dawn, grow bright*
lectīcīs: lectīca *sedan-chair*
Tiberis *river Tiber*
saccāriīs: saccārius *docker, dock-worker*
expōnēbātur: expōnere *unload*
catēnīs: catēna *chain*
modo *just*
sarcinae *bags, luggage*
ortō: ortus *having risen*
Subūram: Subūra *the Subura (noisy and crowded district north of forum)*
obstupefacta est: obstupefacere *amaze, stun*
mendīcī: mendīcus *beggar*
compita: compitum *crossroads*
porrigēbant: porrigere *stretch out*
crepidāriīs: crepidārius *shoemaker*
ferrāriīs: ferrārius *blacksmith*
excūdēbantur: excūdere *forge, hammer out*
fabrīs: faber *carpenter, workman*
procācibus: procāx *impudent, impolite*
appellāvērunt: appellāre *call out to*
ruptīs: rumpere *break, split*
lutum *mud*
dēmovēbant: dēmovēre *move out of way*

When you have read section I of this story, answer the questions at
the end of the section.

salūtātiō

I

prīmā hōrā clientēs ante domum Hateriī conveniēbant. omnēs,
oculīs in iānuam dēfīxīs, patrōnī favōrem exspectābant. aliī
beneficium, aliī sportulam spērābant. puella, servō adstante, in
extrēmā parte multitūdinis cōnstitit; ignāra mōrum Rōmānōrum,
in animō volvēbat cūr tot hominēs illā hōrā ibi stārent.   5
    iānuā subitō apertā, in līmine appāruit praecō. corpus eius erat
ingēns et obēsum, vultus superbus, oculī malignī. clientēs, praecōne
vīsō, clāmāre statim coepērunt. eum ōrāvērunt ut sē ad patrōnum
admitteret. ille tamen superbē circumspectāvit neque quicquam
prīmō dīxit.   10
    omnibus tandem silentibus, praecō ita coepit:
    'dominus noster, Quīntus Haterius Latrōniānus, ratiōnēs suās

subdūcit. iubet igitur trēs cīvēs ratiōnibus testēs subscrībere. cēdite
C. Iūliō Alexandrō, C. Memmiō Prīmō, L. Venūlēiō Aprōniānō.'
quī igitur, audītīs nōminibus suīs, alacriter prōgressī domum   15
intrāvērunt. cēterī autem, oculīs in vultum praecōnis dēfīxīs, spē
favōris manēbant.
'ad cēnam', inquit praecō, 'Haterius invītat L. Volusium
Maeciānum et M. Licinium Prīvātum. Maeciānus et Prīvātus
decimā hōrā redīre iubentur. nunc autem cēdite aliīs! cēdite   20
architectō C. Rabīriō Maximō! cēdite T. Claudiō Papīriō!'
dum illī per iānuam intrant, cēterīs nūntiāvit praecō:
'vōs omnēs iubet Haterius tertiā hōrā sē ad forum dēdūcere.'
hīs verbīs dictīs, paucōs dēnāriōs in turbam sparsit. clientēs, nē
sportulam āmitterent, dēnāriōs rapere temptāvērunt. inter sē   25
vehementer certābant. intereā puella immōta stābat, hōc
spectāculō attonita.

salūtātiō *the morning visit (paid by clients to patron)*	malignī: malignus *spiteful*
	superbē *arrogantly*
sportulam: sportula *handout (gift of food or money)*	ratiōnēs . . . subdūcit: ratiōnēs subdūcere *draw up accounts, write up accounts*
extrēmā parte: extrēma pars *edge*	subscrībere *sign*
līmine: līmen *threshold, doorway*	alacriter *eagerly*
praecō *herald*	dēdūcere *escort*

1 At what time of day did these events take place?
2 Where did the girl stand? What puzzled her?
3 Who was seen on the threshold when the door opened? Describe
   him. What did the clients do when they caught sight of him?
4 Why do you think the herald remained silent at first?
5 How can we tell that all the clients mentioned in line 14 are
   Roman citizens? How can we tell that none of them is a freedman
   of Haterius?
6 What is the effect of the word order in lines 18–19 ('ad
   cēnam . . . Haterius invītat . . . et M. Licinium Prīvātum')?
7 In the herald's announcements, find two examples of small tasks
   that clients have to perform for their patrons, and one example of
   a favour granted by patrons to clients.
8 Why do you think the herald scattered the coins among the crowd
   (line 24) rather than handing the money over in any other way?

II

iānuā tandem clausā, abīre clientēs coepērunt. aliī dēnāriīs collēctīs
abiērunt ut cibum sibi suīsque emerent; aliī spē pecūniae dēiectī
invītī discessērunt. Haterium praecōnemque vituperābant.

deinde servō puella imperāvit ut iānuam pulsāret. praecōnī
regressō servus,   5
'ecce!' inquit. 'domina mea, Euphrosynē, adest.'

'abī, sceleste! nēmō alius hodiē admittitur', respondit praecō
superbā vōce.

'sed domina mea est philosopha Graeca doctissima', inquit
servus. 'hūc missa est ā Quīntō Hateriō Chrȳsogonō ipsō, Hateriī 10
lībertō, quī Athēnīs habitat.'

'īnsānīvit igitur Chrȳsogonus', respondit praecō. 'odiō sunt
omnēs philosophī Hateriō! redeundum vōbīs est Athēnās unde
missī estis.'

servus arrogantiā praecōnis īrātus, nihilōminus perstitit.   15 'sed Eryllus', inquit, 'quī est Hateriō arbiter ēlegantiae, epistulam ad Chrȳsogonum scrīpsit in quā eum rogāvit ut philosopham hūc mitteret. ergō adsumus!'

hīs verbīs audītīs, praecō, quī Eryllum haudquāquam amābat, magnā vōce, 20
'Eryllus!' inquit. 'quis est Eryllus? meus dominus Haterius est, nōn Eryllus! abī!'

haec locūtus servum in lutum dēpulit, iānuamque clausit. Euphrosynē, simulatque servum humī iacentem vīdit, eius īram lēnīre temptāvit. 25

'nōlī', inquit, 'mentem tuam vexāre. nōs decet rēs adversās aequō animō ferre. nōbīs crās reveniendum est.'

suīs: suī *their families*
spē . . . dēiectī *disappointed in their hope*
philosopha *(female) philosopher*
Athēnīs *at Athens*
odiō sunt: odiō esse *be hateful*
redeundum vōbīs est *you must return*
nihilōminus *nevertheless*
perstitit: perstāre *persist*
arbiter *expert, judge*
ēlegantiae: ēlegantia *good taste*
ergō *therefore*
dēpulit: dēpellere *push down*
mentem: mēns *mind*
aequō animō *calmly, in a calm spirit*

About the language

1   Study the following pair of sentences:

mīlitēs discessērunt.
The soldiers departed.

urbe captā, mīlitēs discessērunt.
With the city having been captured, the soldiers departed.

The phrase in heavy print is made up of a noun ('urbe') and participle ('captā') in the *ablative* case. Phrases of this kind are known as *ablative absolute* phrases, and are very common in Latin.

2   Ablative absolute phrases càn be translated in many different ways. For instance, the example in paragraph 1 might be translated:

When the city had been captured, the soldiers departed.
or, After the city was captured, the soldiers departed.

3   Further examples:

1   arcū dēdicātō, cīvēs domum rediērunt.
2   pecūniā āmissā, ancilla lacrimāre coepit.
3   victimīs sacrificātīs, haruspex ōmina nūntiāvit.
4   duce interfectō, hostēs dēspērābant.
5   mercātor, clāmōribus audītīs, ē lectō perterritus surrēxit.
6   senātor, hāc sententiā dictā, cōnsēdit.

4 In each of the examples above, the participle in the ablative absolute phrase is a perfect passive participle. Ablative absolute phrases can also be formed with present participles. For example:

omnibus tacentibus, lībertus nōmina recitāvit.
With everyone being quiet, the freedman read out the names.
  or, in more natural English:
When everyone was quiet, the freedman read out the names.

Further examples:

1 custōdibus dormientibus, captīvī effūgērunt.
2 pompā per viās prōcēdente, spectātōrēs vehementer plausērunt.
3 Imperātor, sacerdōtibus adstantibus, precēs dīvō Titō obtulit.

Ablative absolute phrases can also be formed with perfect active participles. For example:

dominō ēgressō, servī garrīre coepērunt.
With the master having gone out, the slaves began to chatter.
  or, in more natural English:
After the master had gone out, the slaves began to chatter.

Further examples:

4 mercātōre profectō, rēs dīra accidit.
5 nūntiīs ā Britanniā regressīs, imperātor senātōrēs arcessīvit.
6 cōnsule haec locūtō, omnēs cīvēs attonitī erant.

Practising the language

1 Study the way in which the following verbs are formed, and give the meaning of the untranslated ones:

īre	abīre	circumīre	inīre
go		go round	
dūcere	abdūcere	circumdūcere	indūcere
lead			lead in
ferre	auferre	circumferre	īnferre
carry, bring	carry away		

Give the meaning of the following compound verbs:

abicere, āvertere, abesse;
circumstāre, circumvenīre, circumspectāre, circumpōnere;
inesse, inicere, īnsilīre, īnfundere, incurrere, immittere, irrumpere.

2 Complete each sentence with the right word and then translate.

1 multī leōnēs in Āfricā quotannīs . . . . . . (capitur, capiuntur)
2 ecce! ille senex ā latrōnibus . . . . . . (petitur, petuntur)
3 Haterius ā clientibus nunc . . . . . . (salūtātur, salūtantur)
4 mīlitēs in ōrdinēs longōs ā centuriōnibus . . . . . . (īnstruēbātur, īnstruēbantur)
5 oppidum ā barbarīs ferōcibus . . . . . . (oppugnābātur, oppugnābantur)
6 victimae ā sacerdōte . . . . . . (ēligēbātur, ēligēbantur)

3 Complete each sentence with the most suitable word from the list below, and then translate.

portābantur, fraude, vītārent, adeptī, morbō, abēgisset

1 puerī in fossam dēsiluērunt ut perīculum . . . . . .
2 Haterius, ... Salviī dēceptus, cōnsēnsit.
3 multae amphorae in triclīnium . . . . . .
4 senex, ... gravī afflīctus, medicum arcessīvit.
5 praecō, cum Euphrosynēn servumque . . . . ., iānuam clausit.
6 clientēs, sportulam . . . . ., abiērunt.

About the language

1 In Stage 27, you met examples of indirect commands used with 'ut':

imperāvit nūntiīs ut redīrent.
He ordered the messengers that they should return.
  or, in more natural English:
He ordered the messengers to return.

2 From Stage 29 onwards, you have met examples of indirect commands used with the word 'nē':

imperāvit nūntiīs nē redīrent.
He ordered the messengers that they should not return.
  or, in more natural English:
He ordered the messengers not to return.

Further examples:

1 haruspex iuvenem monuit nē nāvigāret.
2 fēminae mīlitēs ōrāvērunt nē līberōs interficerent.
3 mercātor amīcō persuāsit nē vīllam vēnderet.

3 You have also met sentences in which 'nē' is used with a purpose clause:

senex pecūniam cēlāvit nē fūrēs eam invenīrent.
The old man hid the money so that the thieves should not find it.
or, The old man hid the money lest the thieves should find it.

Further examples:

1 per viās celeriter contendēbāmus nē tardī ad arcum advenīrēmus.
2 in fossā latēbam nē hostēs mē cōnspicerent.
3 imperātor multum frūmentum ab Aegyptō importāvit nē cīvēs famē perīrent.

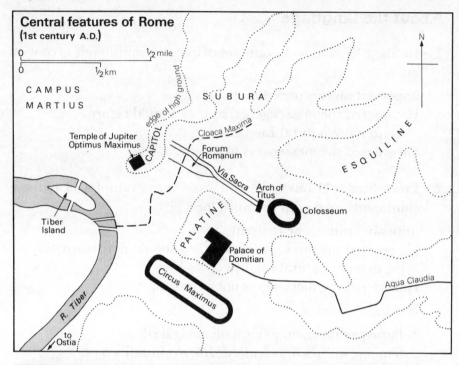

Central features of Rome
(1st century A.D.)

0 ——————— ½ mile
0 ——— ½ km

CAMPUS
MARTIUS

SUBURA

Temple of Jupiter
Optimus Maximus

CAPITOL

Cloaca Maxima

Forum
Romanum

Via Sacra

Arch of
Titus

Colosseum

ESQUILINE

Tiber
Island

PALATINE

Palace of
Domitian

Circus Maximus

R. Tiber

Aqua Claudia

to
Ostia

N

The city of Rome

The city of Rome grew up in a very unplanned and unsystematic way, quite different from the neat grid-pattern of other Roman towns. It was also an extremely crowded city, as can be seen by comparing its approximate area and population with those of two modern metropolitan districts in America and Britain:

	population	*area (sq. miles)*
Los Angeles	2,970,000	465
Greater Manchester	2,770,000	379
Rome (1st century A.D.)	1,000,000 *approx.*	8

The city was bounded on the western side by the river Tiber. Ships brought goods up the Tiber from the coastal port of Ostia to the docks and riverside markets. Further upstream, beyond the wharves and warehouses, the river was divided for a short stretch by the Tiber Island (īnsula Tiberīna). This elongated island, shown in the picture on p.43, had been built up to look like a ship sailing the river, complete with an ornamental prow (rōstrum); it contained a temple of Aesculapius, the god of healing, to which many invalids came in the hope of a cure.

In the story on p.46, Euphrosyne and her slave disembark near the Tiber Island and then move off north-eastwards. Their route could have taken them round the lower slopes of the Capitol and through the forum Romanum (described in Stage 29), passing the Palatine hill where the Emperor Domitian had his palace.

Euphrosyne and the slave would then have continued through the Subura, a densely populated district north of the forum, full of shops and large blocks of flats (īnsulae). Its inhabitants were mostly

Modern tenement blocks in the area of the Subura incorporating ancient walls, which show that the road still runs on the original line down the hill.

poor and some very poor indeed; they included barbers, shoemakers, butchers, weavers, blacksmiths, vegetable sellers, prostitutes and thieves. Several Roman writers refer to the Subura, and give a vivid impression of its noise, its dirt and its crowds. The following passage from Juvenal describes a street which might easily be in the Subura:

> We hurry on, but the way's blocked; there's a tidal wave of people in front, and we're pushed and prodded from behind. One man digs me with his elbow, another with the pole of a sedan-chair; somebody catches me on the head with a plank, and somebody else with a wine-barrel. My legs are plastered with mud, my feet are trodden on by all and sundry, and a soldier is sticking the nail of his boot in my toe.

Many rich and aristocratic Romans settled in the district of the Esquiline hill, which lay to the east of the Subura. Here they could enjoy peace and seclusion in huge mansions, surrounded by colonnaded gardens and landscaped parks which contrasted very sharply with the Subura's slums and crowded tenement blocks. In the stories of Unit IIIB, Haterius' house, where Euphrosyne's journey ended, is imagined as being on the Esquiline.

Among the well-known landmarks of Rome were the Circus Maximus (south of the Palatine), where chariot-races were held, the Colosseum (see p. 102), which lay between the Esquiline and the eastern end of the Sacred Way, and the Campus Martius on the western side of the city, formerly an army training area, which now provided some much-needed open space for the general population.

Crossing the city in various directions were the aqueducts, which brought water into the city at the rate of 900 million litres (200 million gallons) a day. The houses of the rich citizens were usually connected to this supply by means of pipes which brought water directly into their storage tanks; the poorer people had to collect their fresh water from public fountains on street corners. The city also possessed a very advanced system of drains and sewers: a complicated network of underground channels carried sewage and waste water from the larger private houses, public baths, fountains

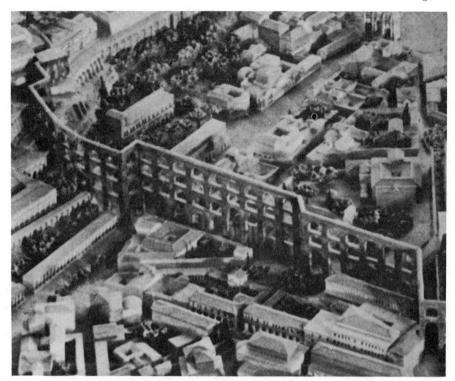

Model of the Aqua Claudia reaching the Palatine.

and lavatories to the central drain (Cloāca Maxima), which emptied into the Tiber.

There were many hazards and discomforts for the inhabitants of Rome. As we have seen in Stage 30 (page 41), fires were frequent and the insulae in the slums were often jerry-built and liable to collapse. The overcrowding and congestion in the streets have already been mentioned above; wheeled traffic was banned from the city centre during the hours of daylight, but blockages were still caused by the wagons of builders like Haterius, which were exempt from the ban. Disease was an ever-present danger in the overcrowded poorer quarters; crime and violence were commonplace in the unlit streets at night. Rome was a city of contrasts, in which splendour and squalor were often found side by side; it could be both an exciting and an unpleasant place to live.

Patronage

The story on pages 48–51 shows one aspect of Roman society known as patronage, in which a patron (patrōnus) gave help and protection to others less rich or powerful than himself, who performed various services for him in return.

There were many different types of patronage, but all were based on the same principle, namely that the patron gave assistance and received service. If the emperor nominated a senator to be one of the next year's consuls, this would be an example of patronage. A merchant might be introduced by his patron to some useful business contacts; a poet's patron might arrange for the poet to recite his work to an audience, or provide him with money or presents, sometimes on a very generous scale. In each case, the patron would expect not only gratitude but favours in return. A poet, for example, would praise the patron in his poetry; the Romans would regard this not as sickly flattery, but as a normal and proper thing to do.

The letters written by Pliny often give us glimpses of patronage in operation. Once, when Pliny was asked to speak in a case in court, he agreed on condition that a young friend of his, who had plenty of ability but had not yet had any chance to show how good he was, should be allowed to make a speech too. And when Pliny's friend Erucius stood as an election candidate, Pliny wrote to an influential ex-consul (and no doubt to other people too), asking him to support Erucius and persuade others to do the same. Pliny was also a patron of his home-town Comum in north Italy, and of the little town of Tifernum-on-Tiber. He gave generous gifts of buildings and money to both places.

But the commonest type of patronage was the type illustrated on pages 48–51, in which the patron looked after a number of poorer people who depended heavily on him for support, employment or even survival. They were known as clients (clientēs). A client was expected to present himself at his patron's house each day for the 'salūtātiō' or early morning ceremony of greeting, at which he received a gift known as the 'sportula'. In the past, the sportula had consisted of a little basket of food, but by Domitian's time it was normally money; the standard amount was fixed by custom at 6¼ sesterces. A client was expected to dress formally in a toga for the salutatio. He also had to address his patron as 'domine'; the poet Martial complains that when he once forgot to do this, the patron punished him by giving him no sportula.

In addition to the sportula, the client might receive help of other kinds from his patron. His patron might advise him if he was in trouble, give him occasional presents, perhaps find him employment or speak on his behalf in court. Once in a while, clients might be invited to dinner at their patron's house. At these dinners, as we know from the angry comments of several Roman writers, some patrons served two different qualities of food and wine: a superior quality for themselves and their close friends, and a poor one for the clients. Some patrons did this to save money, others to make it clear that they regarded their clients as inferiors.

In return for his help a patron would expect his clients not only to attend the salutatio, but also to perform various tasks and errands for him. For example, he might require some of them to escort him when he went to the forum on official business, or to witness the signing of a legal document, or to lead the applause if he made a public speech in court or elsewhere, or to help him at election time. It seems likely that for many clients their duties were not difficult but could be boring and time-consuming.

Both patrons and clients had something to gain from the system. The government did not provide any state assistance or relief for the poor, apart from distributions of free grain or occasionally money, and so a patron might be a client's chief means of support. The main advantage for the patron was that he was able to call on the services of his clients when he needed them; and to have a large number of clients was good for his prestige and status.

One special type of patron–client relationship (which we shall see more of in Stage 34) should be mentioned: the relationship between an ex-master and his former slave. When a slave was set free, he automatically became a client of his ex-master, and his ex-master became his patron. The word 'patrōnus' is sometimes used with the

meaning 'ex-master' as well as the meaning 'patron'.
One man could be the patron of another who in turn was the
patron of somebody else. The following diagram shows how several
people could be linked by patronage:

EMPEROR nominates SALVIUS to an important priesthood

SALVIUS obtains building contract for HATERIUS

HATERIUS orders distribution of sportula to CLIENTS

The emperor has no patron. He is the most powerful patron of all.

Words and phrases checklist

altus, alta, altum – high, deep
angustus, angusta, angustum
    – narrow
ante – before, in front of
catēna, catēnae – chain
cliēns, clientis – client
dux, ducis – leader
favor, favōris – favour
fraus, fraudis – trick
haudquāquam – not at all
īdem, eadem, idem – the same
mōs, mōris – custom
neglegō, neglegere, neglēxī,
    neglēctus – neglect
ōrō, ōrāre, ōrāvī – beg
patrōnus, patrōnī – patron
praecō, praecōnis – herald
praetereō, praeterīre, praeteriī
    – pass by, go past
prōgressus, prōgressa,
    prōgressum – having
    advanced

pūblicus, pūblica, pūblicum –
    public
ratiōnēs, ratiōnum – accounts
reficiō, reficere, refēcī, refectus
    – repair
secō, secāre, secuī, sectus – cut
serēnus, serēna, serēnum –
    calm, clear
spērō, spērāre, spērāvī – hope,
    expect
superbus, superba, superbum
    – arrogant, proud
tempus, temporis – time
ubīque – everywhere
vehō, vehere, vexī, vectus –
    carry
vinciō, vincīre, vīnxī, vīnctus –
    bind, tie up
volvō, volvere, volvī, volūtus –
    turn
  in animō volvere – wonder,
    turn over in the mind
vultus, vultūs – expression, face

Euphrosynē

Euphrosynē revocāta

postrīdiē Euphrosynē domum
Hateriī regressa est. iterum tamen
praecō eam verbīs dūrīs abēgit.

servus eam hortātus est ut praecōnem
dōnīs corrumperet; sed Euphrosynē   5
ab eiusmodī ambitiōne abhorruit.

septem continuōs diēs ā praecōne
abācta, Euphrosynē dēnique in
Graeciam redīre cōnstituit. hōc
cōnsiliō captō, ad flūmen Tiberim   10
ut nāvem cōnscenderet profecta est.

eōdem diē quō Euphrosynē discēdere
cōnstituit, celebrābat Haterius diem
nātālem. grātulātiōnibus clientium
acceptīs, ōtiōsus in hortō sedēbat, in   15
umbrā ingentis laurī. subitō Eryllus
hortum ingressus est.

revocāta: revocāre *recall, call back*
regressa est *returned*
hortātus est *urged*
eiusmodī *of that kind*
ambitiōne: ambitiō *bribery, corruption*

abācta: abigere *drive away*
profecta est *set out*
laurī: laurus *laurel tree*
ingressus est *entered*

Eryllus:	domine! omnia quae mandāvistī parāta sunt. centum amīcī et clientēs ad cēnam invītātī sunt. iussī coquum cibum sūmptuōsum parāre, cellāriumque vīnum 20 Falernum veterrimum dēprōmere. nihil neglēctum est.
Haterius:	nōnne petauristāriōs condūxistī? hercle! quam mē dēlectant petauristāriī!
Eryllus:	quid dīcis, domine? hominēs eiusmodī cīvibus urbānīs 25 nōn placent. nunc philosophīs favet optimus quisque.
Haterius:	īnsānīs, Erylle! nam philosophī sunt senēs sevērī. neque saltāre neque circulōs trānsilīre possunt.
Eryllus:	at domine, aliquid melius quam philosophum adeptus sum. mē enim auctōre, philosopha quaedam, puella 30 pulcherrima, hūc invītāta est. ā Chrȳsogonō Athēnīs missa est.
Haterius:	philosopham mīsit Chrȳsogonus? optimē fēcistī, Erylle! philosopham nē Imperātor quidem habet. sed ubi est haec philosopha quam adeptus es? 35
Eryllus:	iamdūdum eam anxius exspectō. fortasse iste praecō, homō summae stultitiae, eam nōn admīsit.
Haterius:	arcesse hūc praecōnem!

ubi praecō ingressus est, Haterius rogāvit utrum philosopham abēgisset necne. poenās maximās eī minātus est. praecō, verbīs 40 dominī perterritus, palluit; tōtā rē nārrātā, veniam ōrāvit.

praecō:	domine, ignōsce mihi! nesciēbam quantum tū philosophīs favērēs. illa philosopha, quam ignārus abēgī, ad flūmen profecta est ut nāvem cōnscenderet.
Haterius:	abī statim, caudex! festīnā ad Tiberim! nōlī umquam 45 revenīre nisi cum philosophā!

domō ēgressus, praecō per viās contendit. ad flūmen cum advēnisset, Euphrosynēn in nāvem cōnscēnsūram cōnspexit. magnā vōce eam appellāvit. Euphrosynē, nōmine audītō, conversa est. 50

praecō:	ignōsce mihi, Euphrosynē doctissima! nōlī discēdere! necesse est tibi domum Hateriī mēcum prōcēdere.

Euphrosynē: cūr mē revocās? odiō sunt omnēs philosophī Hateriō,
ut tū ipse dīxistī. Athēnās igitur nunc redeō. valē!

deinde praecō, effūsīs lacrimīs, eam identidem ōrāvit nē discēderet. 55
diū Euphrosynē perstitit; dēnique, precibus lacrimīsque eius
permōta, domum Hateriī regressa est.

veterrimum: vetus *old*
dēprōmere *bring out*
petauristāriōs: petauristārius *acrobat*
optimus quisque *all the best people*
sevērī: sevērus *severe, strict*
circulōs: circulus *hoop*
trānsilīre *jump through*
at *but*
adeptus sum *I have obtained*
mē . . . auctōre *at my suggestion*
quaedam: quīdam *a certain*
iamdūdum *for a long time*
utrum . . . necne *whether . . . or not*
minātus est *threatened*
ignōsce: ignōscere *forgive*
Euphrosynēn *Greek accusative of* Euphrosynē
cōnscēnsūram: cōnscēnsūrus *about to go on board*
effūsīs lacrimīs *bursting into tears*

cēna Hateriī

nōnā hōrā amīcī clientēsque, quōs Haterius invītāverat ut sēcum
diem nātālem celebrārent, triclīnium ingrediēbantur. inter eōs
aderant fīliī lībertōrum quī humilī locō nātī magnās opēs adeptī
erant. aderant quoque nōnnūllī senātōrēs quī inopiā oppressī
favōrem Hateriī conciliāre cōnābantur.   5
    proximus Haterium recumbēbat T. Flāvius Sabīnus cōnsul, vir
summae auctōritātis. Haterius blandīs et mollibus verbīs Sabīnum
adloquēbātur, ut favōrem eius conciliāret. ipse in prīmō locō
recumbēbat. pulvīnīs Tyriīs innītēbātur; ānulōs gerēbat aureōs quī
gemmīs fulgēbant; dentēs spīnā argenteā perfodiēbat.   1(
    intereā duo Aethiopes triclīnium ingrediēbantur. lancem
ingentem ferēbant, in quā positus erat aper tōtus. statim coquus,
quī Aethiopas in triclīnium secūtus erat, ad lancem prōgressus est
ut aprum scinderet. aprō perītē scissō, multae avēs statim
ēvolāvērunt suāviter pīpiantēs. convīvae, cum vīdissent quid   1.
coquus parāvisset, eius artem vehementer laudāvērunt. quā rē
dēlectātus, Haterius servīs imperāvit ut amphorās vīnī Falernī
īnferrent. amphorīs inlātīs, cellārius titulōs quī īnfīxī erant magnā
vōce recitāvit, 'Falernum Hateriānum, vīnum centum annōrum!'
tum vīnum in pōcula servī īnfundere coepērunt.   2
    convīvīs laetissimē bibentibus, poposcit Haterius silentium.
spectāculum novum pollicitus est. omnēs convīvae in animō
volvēbant quāle spectāculum Haterius ēditūrus esset. ille rīdēns
digitīs concrepuit. hōc signō datō, Eryllus ē triclīniō ēgressus est.
    appāruērunt in līmine duo tubicinēs. tubās vehementer   2
īnflāvērunt. tum Eryllus Euphrosynēn in triclīnium dūxit.
convīvae, simulatque eam vīdērunt, fōrmam eius valdē admīrātī
sunt.
    Haterius rīdēns Euphrosynēn rogāvit ut sēcum in lectō
cōnsīderet. deinde convīvās adlocūtus est.   3
    'haec puella', inquit glōriāns, 'est philosopha doctissima, nōmine

Euphrosynē. iussū meō hūc vēnit Athēnīs, ubi habitant philosophī
nōtissimī. illa nōbīs dīligenter audienda est.'
   tum ad eam versus,
   'nōbīs placet, mea Euphrosynē', inquit, 'ā tē aliquid philosophiae   35
discere.'

ingrediēbantur *were entering*	pīpiantēs: pīpiāre *chirp*
inopiā: inopia *poverty*	convīvae: convīva *guest*
cōnābantur *were trying*	titulōs: titulus *label*
proximus *next to*	īnfīxī erant: īnfīgere *fasten onto*
adloquēbātur *was addressing*	īnfundere *pour into*
pulvīnīs: pulvīnus *cushion*	pollicitus est *promised*
Tyriīs: Tyrius *Tyrian (coloured with*	editūrus *going to put on, going to present*
dye from city of Tyre)	digitīs: digitus *finger*
innītēbātur *was leaning, was resting*	concrepuit: concrepāre *snap*
spīnā: spīna *toothpick*	fōrmam: fōrma *beauty, appearance*
perfodiēbat: perfodere *pick*	admīrātī sunt *admired*
lancem: lānx *dish*	adlocūtus est *addressed*
scinderet: scindere *carve, cut open*	glōriāns *boasting, boastfully*

About the language

1 Study the following examples:

clientēs pecūniam rapere **cōnābantur.**

The clients were trying to grab the money.

praecō tandem **locūtus est**. At last the herald spoke.

Notice the form and meaning of the words in heavy print. Each verb has a *passive ending* ('-bantur', '-tus est') but an *active meaning* ('they were trying', 'he spoke'). Verbs of this kind are known as *deponent* verbs.

2 Study the following forms of two common deponent verbs:

present

cōnātur	he tries	loquitur	he speaks
cōnantur	they try	loquuntur	they speak

imperfect

cōnābātur	he was trying	loquēbātur	he was speaking
cōnābantur	they were trying	loquēbantur	they were speaking

perfect

cōnātus est	he (has) tried	locūtus est	he spoke, he has spoken
cōnātī sunt	they (have) tried	locūtī sunt	they spoke, they have spoken

pluperfect

cōnātus erat	he had tried	locūtus erat	he had spoken
cōnātī erant	they had tried	locūtī erant	they had spoken

3 Further examples:

1 spectātōrēs dē arcū novō loquēbantur.
2 captīvus effugere cōnātus est.
3 sacerdōs ē templō ēgrediēbātur.
4 fabrī puellam cōnspicātī sunt.
5 sequēbantur; ingressus est; precātur; regrediuntur;
  profectī erant; suspicātus erat.

4 You have already met the *perfect participles* of several deponent verbs. For example:

adeptus   having obtained
hortātus   having encouraged
regressus   having returned

Compare them with the perfect participles of some ordinary verbs (i.e. verbs which are not deponent):

deponent		*ordinary*	
adeptus	having obtained	dēceptus	having been deceived
hortātus	having encouraged	laudātus	having been praised
regressus	having returned	missus	having been sent

Notice that the perfect participle of a deponent verb has an *active* meaning; the perfect participle of an ordinary verb has a *passive* meaning.

5 Further examples of perfect participles of deponent and ordinary verbs:

deponent	*ordinary*
cōnspicātus	portātus
ingressus	iussus
profectus	afflīctus
locūtus	audītus
cōnātus	vulnerātus

When you have read this story, answer the two questions at the end.

philosophia

Euphrosynē convīvās, quī avidē spectābant, sīc adlocūta est:
'prīmum, fābula brevis mihi nārranda est. ōlim fuit homō pauper.'
'quid est pauper?' rogāvit cōnsul Sabīnus, quī mīlle servōs habēbat.
quibus verbīs audītīs, omnēs plausērunt, iocō dēlectātī. Euphrosynē autem, convīvīs tandem silentibus,
'hic pauper', inquit, 'fundum parvum, uxōrem optimam, līberōs cārissimōs habēbat. strēnuē in fundō labōrāre solēbat ut sibi suīsque cibum praebēret.'
'scīlicet īnsānus erat', exclāmāvit Apollōnius, quī erat homō ignāvissimus. 'nēmō nisi īnsānus labōrat.'
cui respondit Euphrosynē vōce serēnā,
'omnibus autem labōrandum est. etiam eī quī spē favōris cēnās magistrātibus dant, rē vērā labōrant.'
quō audītō, Haterius ērubuit; cēterī, verbīs Euphrosynēs obstupefactī, tacēbant. deinde Euphrosynē,
'pauper', inquit, 'neque dīvitiās neque honōrēs cupiēbat. numquam nimium edēbat nec nimium bibēbat. in omnibus vītae partibus moderātus ac temperāns esse cōnābātur.'
L. Baebius Crispus senātor exclāmāvit,
'scīlicet avārus erat! nōn laudandus est nōbīs sed culpandus. Haterius noster tamen maximē laudandus est quod amīcīs sūmptuōsās cēnās semper praebet.'
huic Baebiī sententiae omnēs plausērunt. Haterius, plausū audītō, oblītus philosophiae servīs imperāvit ut plūs vīnī convīvīs offerrent. Euphrosynē tamen haec addidit,
'at pauper multōs cāsūs passus est. līberōs enim et uxōrem āmīsit, ubi afflīxit eōs morbus gravissimus; fundum āmīsit, ubi mīlitēs eum dīripuērunt; lībertātem āmīsit, ubi ipse in servitūtem ā mīlitibus vēnditus est. nihilōminus, quia Stōicus erat, rēs adversās semper

Relief showing a farmer taking his produce to market. At the top left is a little shrine with a god standing in the archway.

aequō animō patiēbātur; neque deōs neque hominēs dētestābātur. dēnique senectūte labōribusque cōnfectus, tranquillē mortuus est. ille pauper, quem hominēs miserrimum exīstimābant, rē vērā fēlīx erat.'   35

philosophia *philosophy*
suīs: suī *his family*
scīlicet *obviously*
rē vērā *in fact, truly*
Euphrosynēs *Greek genitive of*
  Euphrosynē
edēbat: edere *eat*
moderātus *restrained, moderate*
temperāns *temperate, self-controlled*

culpandus: culpāre *blame*
plausū: plausus *applause*
cāsūs: cāsus *misfortune*
Stōicus *Stoic (believer in Stoic philosophy)*
patiēbātur *suffered, endured*
senectūte: senectūs *old age*
tranquillē *peacefully*
exīstimābant: exīstimāre *think, consider*

Haterius cachinnāns 'num fēlīcem eum exīstimās', inquit, 'quī tot cāsūs passus est?'

Hateriō hoc rogantī respondit Euphrosynē,

'id quod locūta sum nōn rēctē intellegis. alia igitur fābula mihi nārranda est. ōlim fuit homō dīves.'

sed cōnsul Sabīnus, quem iam taedēbat fābulārum, exclāmāvit, 'satis philosophiae! age, mea Euphrosynē, dā mihi ōsculum, immo ōscula multa.'

Rabīrius Maximus tamen, quī cum haec audīvisset ēbrius surrēxit,

'sceleste', inquit, 'nōlī eam tangere!'

haec locūtus, pōculum vīnō plēnum in ōs Sabīnī iniēcit.

statim rēs ad pugnam vēnit. pōcula iaciēbantur; lectī ēvertēbantur; togae scindēbantur. aliī Sabīnō, aliī Rabīriō subveniēbant. Haterius hūc illūc currēbat; discordiam compōnere cōnābatur. eum tamen currentem atque ōrantem nēmō animadvertit.

Euphrosynē autem, ad iānuam triclīniī vultū serēnō prōgressa, convīvās pugnantēs ita adlocūta est:

'ēn Rōmānī, dominī orbis terrārum, ventris Venerisque servī!'

quibus verbīs dictīs, ad flūmen Tiberim ut nāvem quaereret profecta est.

rēctē *rightly, properly*
immo *or rather*
compōnere *settle*
animadvertit: animadvertere *notice, take notice of*
orbis terrārum *world*
Veneris: Venus *Venus (goddess of love)*

1 Why was Euphrosyne's philosophy lecture a failure?
2 Look again at Euphrosyne's remark 'ille pauper . . . rē vērā fēlīx erat' (lines 34–5). Was Haterius right to suggest that this is a stupid remark? Or does it have some point?

About the language

1 In Stage 26, you met the gerundive used in sentences like this:

mihi currendum est.   I must run.

2 In Stage 32, you have met more sentences containing gerundives. For example:

mihi fābula nārranda est.   I must tell a story.

Compare this with another way of expressing the same idea:

necesse est mihi fābulam nārrāre.

3 Further examples:

1 mihi epistula scrībenda est.
   (Compare: necesse est mihi epistulam scrībere.)
2 tibi testāmentum faciendum est.
3 nōbīs Haterius vīsitandus est.
4 coquō cēna paranda est.
5 tibi fidēs servanda est.

Practising the language

1 Study the form and meaning of the following verbs and nouns, and give the meaning of the untranslated words:

advenīre	arrive	adventus	arrival
movēre	move	mōtus	movement
plaudere	applaud	plausus	
metuere	be afraid	metus	
cōnspicere		cōnspectus	sight
monēre		monitus	warning
rīdēre		rīsus	
gemere		gemitus	

Give the meaning of the following nouns:

reditus, sonitus, cantus, cōnsēnsus

2   Make up five Latin sentences using some of the words listed below. Write out each sentence and then translate it. Include at least one sentence which does not contain a nominative.

A genitive usually follows the noun it refers to. For example:

amīcī rēgis equum invēnērunt.   The friends of the king found the horse.

amīcī equum rēgis invēnērunt.   The friends found the king's horse.

nominatives	*accusatives*	*genitives*	*verbs*
uxor	domōs	puerōrum	invēnit
servus	nāvēs	rēgis	invēnērunt
filiī	equum	agricolae	custōdiēbat
clientēs	pecūniam	mīlitum	custōdiēbant
lībertus	librum	fēminārum	dēlēbat
amīcī	gemmās	captīvī	dēlēbant
hostēs	corpus	haruspicis	abstulit
dux	pontem	populī Rōmānī	abstulērunt

3   With the help of paragraphs 1 and 2 on page 130 in the Language Information section, complete each sentence by describing the word in heavy print with the correct form of the adjective in brackets, and then translate.

For example: clientēs **patrōnum** . . . . . laudāvērunt. (līberālis)
Answer: clientēs patrōnum līberālem laudāvērunt.
              The clients praised their generous patron.

The gender of the word in heavy print is given after each sentence.

1 nautae **nāvem** . . . . . comparāvērunt. (optimus) (f.)
2 coquus īram **dominī** . . . . . timēbat. (crūdēlis) (m.)
3 mercātor, **itinere** . . . . . dēfessus, in rīpā flūminis cōnsēdit. (longus) (n.)
4 senex testāmentum **amīcō** . . . . . mandāvit. (fidēlis) (m.)
5 centuriō verba **uxōris** . . . . . neglēxit. (īrātus) (f.)
6 **saxa** . . . . . ad arcum ā fabrīs trahēbantur. (gravis) (n.)
7 subitō vōcēs **mīlitum** . . . . . audīvimus. (īnfestus) (m.)
8 Euphrosynē **convīvīs** . . . . . statim respondit. (īnsolēns) (m.)

4 In each pair of sentences, translate sentence 'a'; then change it from a direct command to an indirect command by completing sentence 'b' with an imperfect subjunctive, and translate again.

For example: a pontem incende!
              b centuriō mīlitī imperāvit ut pontem
                 incender... .

Translated and completed, this becomes:
  a pontem incende!   Burn the bridge down!
  b centuriō mīlitī imperāvit ut pontem incenderet.
     The centurion ordered the soldier to burn the bridge down.

The forms of the imperfect subjunctive are given on page 142 in the Language Information section.

1a pecūniam cēlāte!
1b mercātor amīcōs monuit ut pecūniam cēlār... .
2a arcum mihi ostende!
2b puer patrem ōrāvit ut arcum sibi ostender... .
3a iānuam aperīte!
3b imperātor nōbīs imperāvit ut iānuam aperīr... .
4a nōlīte redīre!
4b fēmina barbarīs persuāsit nē redīr... .

In sentences 5 and 6, turn the direct command into an indirect command by adding the necessary words to sentence 'b':

5a cēnam optimam parāte!
5b dominus servīs imperāvit ut . . . . . .
6a epistulam scrībe!
6b frāter mihi persuāsit . . . . . .

About the language

1 Study the following examples:

nunc ego quoque **moritūrus** sum.
Now I, too, am about to die.

nēmō sciēbat quid Haterius **factūrus** esset.
Nobody knew what Haterius was going to do.

praecō puellam vīdit, nāvem **cōnscēnsūram**.
The herald saw the girl about to go on board ship.

The words in heavy print are *future participles*.

2 Further examples:

1 nunc ego vōbīs cēnam splendidam datūrus sum.
2 mīlitēs in animō volvēbant quid centuriō dictūrus esset.
3 convīvae Haterium rogāvērunt num Euphrosynē saltātūra esset.

3 Compare the future participle with the perfect passive participle:

perfect passive participle	*future participle*
portātus	portātūrus
having been carried	about to carry
doctus	doctūrus
having been taught	about to teach
tractus	tractūrus
having been dragged	about to drag
audītus	audītūrus
having been heard	about to hear

Roman society

The following diagram shows one way of dividing up Roman society:

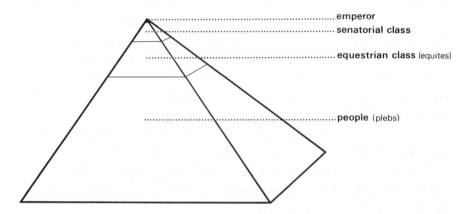

At the top of the pyramid is the emperor. Below him are the men of the senatorial class. Membership of this group was by inheritance (in other words, members' sons were automatically qualified to become members themselves); membership could also be given to an individual by the emperor as a special privilege. A man who was in the senatorial class had the opportunity to follow a political career which could lead (if he was good enough) to high positions such as the command of a legion, the consulship, or the governorship of a province. Both Agricola and Salvius are examples of men who reached high positions of this kind.

Members of the senatorial class also possessed various privileges to emphasise their status: they wore a broad purple stripe on their tunics, sat in special places reserved for them at public ceremonies and entertainments, and were eligible for certain priesthoods and similar honours. To retain their membership, however, men of the senatorial class had to possess 1,000,000 sesterces in money or property. It occasionally happened that a senatorial family's wealth dropped below the 1,000,000-sesterce line. When this happened, the members of the family, like the senators at the party on page 68, were in danger of being expelled from the senatorial class by the 'censors', who had the job of periodically bringing the membership list up to date.

Below the senatorial class are the men of equestrian class or 'equitēs'. The qualification for membership of this class was 400,000 sesterces. The equites could follow a career in government if they wished, at a rather humbler level than the senatorial career; they might, for example, command an auxiliary unit in the army or supervise a province's financial affairs. If they were exceptionally able or lucky, they might rise to the highest positions in an equestrian career, such as the command of the praetorian guard or the governorship of Egypt. Signs of equestrian status included the wearing of a special gold ring, and a narrow stripe on the tunic. A number of equites, like Haterius in the stories in Unit IIIB, were extremely rich – richer in fact than many senators. Some were offered promotion by the emperor into the senatorial class, though not all of them chose to accept.

Below the equites are the ordinary people, or 'plēbs'. As the diagram indicates, they formed the great mass of the Roman population. Some of them earned a reasonably comfortable living as craftsmen or shopkeepers, or ran small businesses. Many depended on casual and irregular employment (as porters, for example, or as temporary labourers on building sites). Others lived in extreme poverty, with nothing to save them from starvation except the help of their patron or the public distribution of free grain made by the emperor's officials to Roman citizens. In general, the plebs were entirely excluded from positions of power and prestige. A few, however, through hard work or luck or their patron's assistance, succeeded in becoming equites or even (more rarely) reaching the senatorial class.

Astrology, philosophy and other beliefs

Many Romans were contented with the official state religion and its rituals of prayer, divination and sacrifice, described in Stage 23. Some, however, found greater satisfaction in other forms of belief, including astrology, philosophy and foreign cults. Many took part in both the state religion and some other kind of worship, without feeling that there was any conflict between the two.

One popular form of belief, which you met in Unit IIB, was astrology. Astrologers claimed that the events in a person's life were controlled by the stars, and that it was possible to forecast the future by studying the positions and movements of stars and planets. The position of the stars at the time of a person's birth was known as a horoscope and regarded as particularly important. Astrology was officially disapproved of, especially if people used it to try to find out when their relatives or acquaintances were going to die, and from time to time all astrologers were banished from Rome. (They were always back again within a few months.) In particular, it was a serious offence to enquire about the horoscope of the emperor. Several emperors, however, were themselves firm believers in astrology and kept private astrologers of their own.

A few Romans, especially those who had come into contact with Greek ideas through education or travel, became interested in philosophy. Philosophy was concerned with such questions as: 'What is the world made of?' 'What happens to us after we die?' 'What is the right way to live?' In particular, a number of Romans were attracted by the philosophy of Stoicism. Stoics believed, like Euphrosyne in the story on pp.72–4, that a man's aim in life should be Virtue (right behaviour) rather than Pleasure. The philosopher Seneca, who taught the Emperor Nero, wrote: 'Virtue stands tall and high like a king, invincible and untiring; Pleasure crawls and grovels like a beggar, weak and feeble. Virtue is found in temples, in the forum and the senate-house, defending the city walls, covered in dust, burnt by the sun, with hands hardened by toil; Pleasure is found skulking in the shadows, lurking in baths and brothels and places which fear the police, soft, flabby and gutless, soaked in scent and wine, with a face pale or painted with cosmetics.'

At the time of the stories in Stage 32, the most important Stoic philosopher in Rome was a Greek named Epictetus. Epictetus had formerly been a slave; the lameness from which he suffered was said to have been caused by brutal treatment at the hands of his master (the Emperor's freedman, Epaphroditus). While still a slave, Epictetus was allowed to attend philosophy lectures, and when he was freed he became a philosophy teacher himself and attracted large audiences.

Stoics tended to disapprove of one-man rule, and to prefer the idea of a republic. They did not think supreme political power should be passed on by inheritance from one ruler to the next, and they thought a ruler should aim to benefit all his subjects, not just a few. As a result of this, at various times during the first century, a number of Roman Stoics challenged the power of the emperor, opposed him in the Senate, or even plotted to kill him. Their efforts were unsuccessful, and they were punished by exile or death.

Relief of Mithras killing the bull, surrounded by the signs of the zodiac.

A ceremony in a temple of Mithras.

Some Romans became followers of foreign cults, especially those that involved dramatic initiation ceremonies or offered hope of life after death. One such cult was the religion of Isis, whose ritual was described in Stage 19. Another was Mithraism, or Mithras-worship. Mithras was a god of light and truth, who triumphed over the forces of evil, and promised life after death to his followers. His powers were summed up in the story of his chief exploit: the capture and killing of a mighty bull, whose blood had the power to give new life. There were seven grades of initiation into Mithraism, each with its own secret ceremony, involving tests and ordeals of various kinds. Lying in a pit formed part of one ceremony; branding may have formed part of another. Mithraism expected high standards of conduct from its followers; it laid great stress on courage and loyalty, and became popular in the army. Nevertheless, it was a rather expensive and exclusive religion; those who were initiated seem to have been mainly army officers (rather than ordinary legionaries) or wealthy businessmen. A number of Mithraic temples have been discovered, including one in London and another at Carrawburgh in Northumberland, close to Hadrian's Wall.

Isis-worship and Mithraism both came to Rome from the east, Isis-worship from Egypt and Mithraism from Persia. From the east, too, came Christianity, which was at first disliked by the Romans and at times was fiercely attacked, but eventually became the official religion of the Roman empire. It will be described more fully in Stage 33.

Words and phrases checklist

addō, addere, addidī, additus – add
adversus, adversa, adversum – hostile, unfavourable
　rēs adversae – misfortune
aequus, aequa, aequum – fair, calm
　aequō animō – calmly, in a calm spirit
appellō, appellāre, appellāvī, appellātus – call, call out to
avis, avis – bird
cāsus, cāsūs – misfortune
compōnō, compōnere, composuī, compositus – put together,
　arrange, settle
cōnātus, cōnāta, cōnātum – having tried
condūcō, condūcere, condūxī, conductus – hire
convertō, convertere, convertī, conversus – turn
effundō, effundere, effūdī, effūsus – pour out
identidem – repeatedly
ignōscō, ignōscere, ignōvī – forgive
labor, labōris – work
lībertās, lībertātis – freedom
nē . . . quidem – not even
nihilōminus – nevertheless
opprimō, opprimere, oppressī, oppressus – crush
ōtiōsus, ōtiōsa, ōtiōsum – idle, on holiday, on vacation
pauper, *gen.* pauperis – poor
permōtus, permōta, permōtum – alarmed, disturbed
profectus, profecta, profectum – having set out
quia – because
quīdam, quaedam, quoddam – one, a certain
scindō, scindere, scidī, scissus – tear, tear up, cut up
secūtus, secūta, secūtum – having followed
strēnuē – hard, energetically
subveniō, subvenīre, subvēnī – help, come to help
sūmptuōsus, sūmptuōsa, sūmptuōsum – expensive, lavish, costly
vērus, vēra, vērum – true, real
　rē vērā – in fact, truly, really

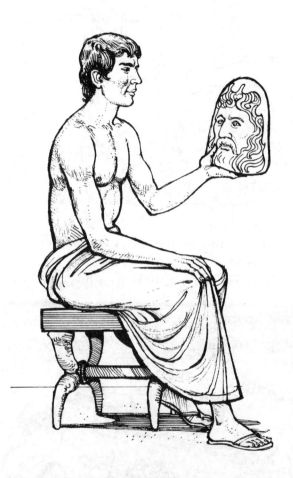

pantomīmus

praecō prīmus:	fābula! fābula optima!
	Paris, pantomīmus nōtissimus, in theātrō crās fābulam aget.
	Myropnous, tībīcen perītissimus, tībiīs cantābit.

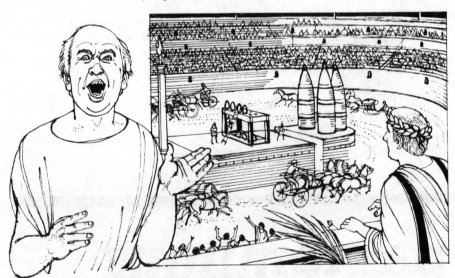

praecō secundus:	lūdī! lūdī magnificī!
	duodecim aurīgae in Circō Maximō crās certābunt.
	Imperātor ipse victōrī praemium dabit.

| praecō tertius: | spectāculum! spectāculum splendidum! quīnquāgintā gladiātōrēs in amphitheātrō Flāviō crās pugnābunt. multus sanguis fluet. |

Tychicus

in hortō Hateriī, fābula agēbātur. Paris, pantomīmus nōtissimus, mortem rēgīnae Dīdōnis imitābātur. aderant multī spectātōrēs quī ad fābulam ā Vitelliā, uxōre Hateriī, invītātī erant. Haterius ipse nōn aderat. labōribus cōnfectus atque spē sacerdōtiī dēiectus, ad vīllam rūsticam abierat ut quiēsceret.   5

Paris mōtibus ēlegantissimīs aptissimīsque dolōrem rēgīnae morientis imitābātur. cum dēnique quasi mortuus prōcubuisset, omnēs spectātōrēs admīrātiōne affectī identidem plaudēbant. aliī flōrēs iactābant; aliī Paridem deum appellābant. surrēxit Paris ut plausum spectātōrum exciperet.   10

| pantomīmus *pantomimus, dancer* | mōtibus: mōtus *movement* |
| imitābātur *was imitating, was miming* | quasi *as if* |

sed priusquam ille plūra ageret, vir quīdam statūrā brevī
vultūque sevērō prōgressus magnā vōce silentium poposcit. oculīs
in eum statim conversīs, spectātōrēs quis esset et quid vellet
rogābant. paucī eum agnōvērunt. Iūdaeus erat, Tychicus nōmine,
cliēns T. Flāviī Clēmentis. Paris ipse fābulā interruptā adeō 15
obstupefactus est ut stāret immōtus. omnīnō ignōrābat quid
Tychicus factūrus esset.

'audīte, ō scelestī!' clāmāvit Tychicus. 'vōs prāvī hunc hominem
tamquam deum adōrātis. sunt tamen nūllī deī praeter ūnum! ūnus
Deus sōlus adōrandus est! hunc Deum quem plērīque vestrum 20
ignōrant, oportet mē nunc vōbīs dēclārāre.'

mussitāre coepērunt spectātōrēs. aliī rogāvērunt utrum Tychicus
iocōs faceret an īnsānīret; aliī servōs arcessīvērunt quī eum ex hortō
ēicerent. Tychicus autem perstitit.

'Deus, ut prophētae nostrī nōbīs praedīxērunt, homō factus est et 25
inter nōs habitāvit. aegrōs sānāvit; evangelium prōnūntiāvit; vītam
aeternam nōbīs pollicitus est. tum in cruce suffīxus, mortuus est et
in sepulcrō positus est. sed tertiō diē resurrēxit et vīvus ā discipulīs

suīs vīsus est. deinde in caelum ascendit, ubi et nunc rēgnat et in
perpetuum rēgnābit.'   30
dum haec Tychicus dēclārat, servī Vitelliae signō datō eum
comprehendērunt. domō eum trahēbant magnā vōce clāmantem:
'mox Dominus noster, rēx glōriae, ad nōs reveniet; ē caelō
dēscendet cum sonitū tubārum, magnō numerō angelōrum
comitante. et vīvōs et mortuōs iūdicābit. nōs Chrīstiānī, sī vītam 35
pūram vīxerimus et eī crēdiderimus, ad caelum ascendēmus. ibi
semper cum Dominō erimus. tū autem, Paris, fīlius diabolī, nisi
vitiīs tuīs dēstiteris, poenās dabis. nūlla erit fuga. nam flammae, ē
caelō missae, tē et omnēs scelestōs dēvorābunt.'
    quae cum prōnūntiāvisset, Tychicus multīs verberibus acceptīs 40
domō ēiectus est. spectātōrum plūrimī eum vehementer dērīdēbant;
paucī tamen, praesertim servī ac lībertī, tacēbant, quod Chrīstiānī
erant ipsī.

priusquam *before*	discipulīs: discipulus *disciple, follower*
statūrā: statūra *height*	caelum *sky, heaven*
interruptā: interrumpere *interrupt*	rēgnat: rēgnāre *reign*
praeter *except*	in perpetuum *for ever*
plērīque vestrum *most of you*	glōriae: glōria *glory*
dēclārāre *declare, proclaim*	angelōrum: angelus *angel*
mussitāre *murmur*	comitante: comitāns *accompanying*
prophētae: prophēta *prophet*	iūdicābit: iūdicāre *judge*
praedīxērunt: praedīcere *foretell, predict*	pūram: pūrus *pure*
evangelium *good news, gospel*	erimus *shall be*
prōnūntiāvit: prōnūntiāre *proclaim, preach*	diabolī: diabolus *devil*
aeternam: aeternus *eternal*	nisi *unless*
cruce: crux *cross*	vitiīs: vitium *sin*
suffīxus: suffīgere *nail, fasten*	verberibus: verber *blow*
resurrēxit: resurgere *rise again*	

When you have read section I of this story, answer the questions at the end of the section.

in aulā Domitiānī

I

in scaenā parvā, quae in aulae Domitiānī ātriō exstrūcta erat, Paris fābulam dē amōre Mārtis et Veneris agēbat. simul pūmiliō, Myropnous nōmine, tībīcen atque amīcus Paridis, suāviter tībiīs cantābat. nūllī aderant spectātōrēs nisi Domitia Augusta, uxor Imperātōris Domitiānī, quae Paridem inter familiārissimōs suōs 5 habēbat. oculīs in eō fīxīs fābulam intentē spectābat. tam mīrābilis, tam perīta ars eius erat ut lacrimās retinēre Domitia vix posset.

subitō servus, nōmine Olympus, quem Domitia iānuam ātriī custōdīre iusserat, ingressus est.

'domina', inquit, 'nōs Epaphrodītum, Augustī lībertum, modo 10 cōnspicātī sumus trānseuntem āream, decem mīlitibus comitantibus. mox hūc intrābit.'

quibus verbīs audītīs, Paris ad Domitiam versus rīsit.

Paris: dēliciae meae! quam fortūnāta es! Epaphrodītus ipse,
           Augustī lībertus, tē vīsitāre cupit.
Domitia: (*adventū Epaphrodītī commōta*) mī Pari, tibi perīculōsum est
           hīc manēre. odiō es Epaphrodītō! sī tē apud mē ille
           invēnerit, poenās certē dabis. iubēbit mīlitēs in carcerem
           tē conicere. fuge!
Paris: cūr fugiendum est? illum psittacum Domitiānī floccī nōn
           faciō.
Domitia: at ego valdē timeō. nam mihi quoque Epaphrodītus est
           inimīcus. iussū eius conclāvia mea saepe īnspiciuntur;
           epistulae meae resignantur; ancillārum meārum fidēs ā
           ministrīs eius temptātur. potestās eius nōn minor est
           quam Imperātōris ipsīus.
Paris: mea columba, dēsine timēre! mē nōn capiet iste
           homunculus. paulīsper abībō.

haec locūtus, columnam proximam celeriter cōnscendit et per
compluvium ēgressus in tēctō sē cēlāvit. Myropnous quoque sē 30
cēlāre cōnstituit. post tapēte quod dē longuriō gravī pendēbat sē
collocāvit. Domitia contrā, quae quamquam perterrita erat in lectō
manēbat vultū compositō, Olympō imperāvit ut aliquōs versūs
recitāret.

simul *at the same time*
tībiīs cantābat: tībiīs cantāre *play on
the pipes*
familiārissimōs: familiāris *close friend*
Augustī lībertum: Augustī lībertus
*freedman of Augustus, freedman
of the emperor*
certē *certainly*
conclāvia: conclāve *room*

īnspiciuntur: īnspicere *search*
resignantur: resignāre *open, unseal*
ministrīs: minister *servant, agent*
temptātur: temptāre *put to the test*
compluvium *compluvium (opening in roof)*
tapēte *tapestry, wall-hanging*
longuriō: longurius *pole*
contrā *on the other hand*
compositō: compositus *composed, steady*

1 Where in the palace did Paris' performance take place? What story was he performing? Who was supplying the musical accompaniment?
2 Who was the only spectator? What effect did Paris' skill have on her?
3 What had the slave Olympus been ordered to do? What news did he bring? What were Domitia's feelings on hearing this news?
4 Domitia mentions three ways in which Epaphroditus and his men are making life unpleasant for her. What are they?
5 Where did (*a*) Paris and (*b*) Myropnous hide?
6 While Paris and Myropnous were hiding, where was Domitia? In what ways did she try to pretend that everything was normal?
7 Judging from this story, especially lines 14–28, what impression do you have of Paris' personality?

II

Olympō suāviter recitante, ingressus est Epaphrodītus. decem mīlitēs eum comitābantur.

Epaphrodītus:	ubi est iste pantomīmus quem impudēns tū amās? ubi eum cēlāvistī?
Domitia:	verba tua nōn intellegō. sōla sum, ut vidēs. hic 5 servus mē versibus dēlectat, nōn Paris.
Epaphrodītus:	(*conversus ad mīlitēs*) quaerite Paridem! festīnāte! omnia īnspicite conclāvia!

mīlitēs igitur conclāvia ācriter perscrūtātī sunt, sed frūstrā.
Paridem nusquam invenīre poterant.   10

Epaphrodītus:	caudicēs! sī Paris effūgerit, vōs poenās dabitis. cūr tēctum nōn perscrūtātī estis? ferte scālās!

quae cum audīvisset Domitia palluit. Myropnous tamen quī per tapēte cautē prōspiciēbat sēcum rīsit; cōnsilium enim callidissimum et audācissimum cēperat. tapēte lēniter manū movēre coepit. mox 15 Epaphrodītus, dum ātrium suspīciōsus circumspectat, mōtum tapētis animadvertit.

Epaphrodītus: ecce! movētur tapēte! latebrās Paridis invēnī! nunc illum capiam.

quibus dictīs, Epaphrodītus ad tapēte cum magnō clāmōre sē 20
praecipitāvit. Myropnous haudquāquam perturbātus, ubi Epaphrodītus appropinquāvit, tapēte magnā vī dētrāxit. dēcidit tapēte, dēcidit longurius. Epaphrodītus, tapētī convolūtus atque simul longuriō percussus, prōcubuit exanimātus. magnopere cachinnāvit Myropnous et exsultāns tībiīs cantāre coepit.   25
    Domitia, quae sē iam ex pavōre recēperat, ad mīlitēs in ātrium cum scālīs regressōs conversa est. eōs iussit Epaphrodītum extrahere. mīlitibus eum extrahentibus Myropnous assem in labra eius quasi mortuī posuit. dēnique Paris per compluvium dēspexit et Epaphrodītō ita valēdīxit: 30
    'hīc iacet Tiberius Claudius Epaphrodītus, Augustī lībertus, longuriō gravī strātus.'

impudēns *shameless*
perscrūtātī sunt *examined*
scālās: scālae *ladders*
suspīciōsus *suspicious*
latebrās: latebrae *hiding-place*
sē praecipitāvit: sē praecipitāre *hurl oneself*
dētrāxit: dētrahere *pull down*
convolūtus: convolvere *entangle*
assem: as *as (small coin)*
dēspexit: dēspicere *look down*
strātus: sternere *lay low*

About the language

1 Study the following examples:

nōlī dēspērāre! amīcus meus tē **servābit**.
Don't give up! My friend will save you.

servī ad urbem heri iērunt; crās **revenient**.
The slaves went to the city yesterday; they will come back tomorrow.

The words in heavy print are in the *future* tense.

2 The first and second conjugations form their future tense in the following way:

first conjugation

portābō	I shall carry
portābis	you will carry
portābit	he will carry
portābimus	we shall carry
portābitis	you will carry
portābunt	they will carry

second conjugation

docēbō	I shall teach
docēbis	you will teach
etc.	

3 The third and fourth conjugations form their future tense in another way:

third conjugation

traham	I shall drag
trahēs	you will drag
trahet	he will drag
trahēmus	we shall drag
trahētis	you will drag
trahent	they will drag

fourth conjugation

audiam	I shall hear
audiēs	you will hear
etc.	

4 Further examples:

1 crās ad Graeciam nāvigābimus.
2 ille mercātor est mendāx; tibi numquam pecūniam reddet.
3 fuge! mīlitēs tē in carcerem conicient!
4 dux noster est vir benignus, quī vōs omnēs līberābit.
5 'quid crās faciēs?' 'ad theātrum ībō.'
6 laudābō; respondēbit; appropinquābunt; rīdēbitis.
7 veniēmus; trādent; dīcam; dormiet.

5 The future tense of 'sum' is as follows:

erō	I shall be	erimus	we shall be
eris	you will be	eritis	you will be
erit	he will be	erunt	they will be

Practising the language

1 Study the form and meaning of the following nouns, and give the meaning of the untranslated ones:

homō	man	homunculus	little man
servus	slave	servulus	little slave
lagōna	bottle	laguncula	
corpus		corpusculum	little body
febris		febricula	slight fever
liber	book	libellus	
ager		agellus	
lapis		lapillus	
fīlia		fīliola	
mēnsa		mēnsula	

The nouns in the right-hand pair of columns are known as *diminutives*.

Give the meaning of the following diminutives:

vīllula, fīliolus, nāvicula, cēnula, ponticulus

Study the following nouns and their diminutives:

sporta	basket	sportula	(1) little basket
			(2) gift for clients (named after the little basket in which it once used to be carried)
cōdex (*often* (1) piece of *spelt* caudex)	wood (2) someone with no more sense than a piece of wood, i.e. fool, blockhead	cōdicillī	(1) wooden writing-tablets (2) codicil (written instructions added to a will)

2 Complete each sentence with the right word and then translate.

1 hīs verbīs . . . . ., Paris aequō animō respondit. (audītīs, portātīs)

2 signō . . . . ., servī Tychicum ēiēcērunt. (victō, datō)

3 cēnā . . . . ., Haterius amīcōs in triclīnium dūxit. (cōnsūmptā, parātā)

4 nāve . . . . ., mercātor dēspērābat. (āmissā, refectā)

5 clientibus . . . . ., praecō iānuam clausit. (dīmissīs, dēpositīs)

6 tergīs . . . . ., hostēs fūgērunt. (īnstrūctīs, conversīs)

3 In each pair of sentences, translate sentence 'a'; then, with the help of page 140 in the Language Information section, express the same idea in a different way by completing sentence 'b' with a passive form, and translate again.

For example: a tabernāriī cibum vēndēbant.
            b cibus ā tabernāriīs . . . . . .
Translated and completed, this becomes:
a tabernāriī cibum vēndēbant.
  The shopkeepers were selling food.
b cibus ā tabernāriīs vēndēbātur.
  Food was being sold by the shopkeepers.

In sentences 1–3, the verbs are in the *imperfect* tense:

1a servī amphorās portābant.
1b amphorae ā servīs . . . . . .
2a Salvius Haterium dēcipiēbat.
2b Haterius ā Salviō . . . . . .
3a barbarī horreum oppugnābant.
3b horreum ā barbarīs . . . . . .

In sentences 4–6, the verbs are in the *present* tense:

4a rhētor puerōs docet.
4b puerī ā rhētore . . . . . .
5a aliquis iānuam aperit.
5b iānua ab aliquō . . . . . .
6a centuriō mīlitēs cōnsistere iubet.
6b mīlitēs ā centuriōne cōnsistere . . . . . .

About the language

1 Study the following example:

sī tē audīverō, respondēbō.
If I hear you, I shall reply.

The replying takes place in the future, so Latin uses the future tense ('respondēbō'). The hearing also takes place in the future, but at a different time: hearing comes before replying. To indicate this difference in time, Latin uses an unusual tense known as the *future perfect* ('audīverō').

2 The forms of the future perfect are as follows:

portāverō   portāverimus
portāveris   portāveritis
portāverit   portāverint

3 The future perfect is often translated by an English present tense, as in the example in paragraph 1.

4 Further examples:

1 sī Epaphrodītus nōs cōnspexerit, mē interficiet.
2 sī dīligenter quaesīveris, pecūniam inveniēs.
3 sī servī bene labōrāverint, eīs praemium dabō.
4 sī mīlitēs vīderō, fugiam.

Christianity

Christianity originated in the Roman province of Judaea, where Jesus Christ was crucified in about A.D.29. It may have reached Rome during the reign of the Emperor Claudius (A.D.41–54). Saint Paul, who was brought to Rome under arrest in about A.D.60, ends one of his letters from Rome by passing on messages of greeting from several Christians living in the city, including some who belong to 'Caesar's house' (the household of the emperor).

The early Christians believed that Jesus had not only risen from the dead and ascended into heaven, but would return again to earth in the fairly near future, in the way described by Tychicus on page 89. The message of Christianity appealed mainly to the poor and the down-trodden, although it also attracted a few of the wealthy and nobly born.

At first the Romans tended to confuse Christianity with Judaism. This is not surprising, since both religions came from Judaea, and both believed that there was only one God. Christians were

The head of Christ from the Hinton St Mary mosaic, Dorset.

generally disliked by the Romans; occasionally they were persecuted (hunted down and punished). The most famous persecution took place in A.D.64 under the Emperor Nero, who treated the Christians as scapegoats for the great fire of Rome. They were condemned to be torn to pieces by wild beasts, or set alight as human torches.

But persecutions like these were not common; the Roman government usually preferred to leave the Christians alone. When Pliny, the Roman governor of Bithynia, asked the Emperor Trajan how he ought to deal with people accused of Christianity, Trajan replied: 'They are not to be hunted down: if they are brought before you and proved guilty, they must be punished, but if any one says that he is *not* a Christian and proves it by saying a prayer to our Roman gods, he must go free, even if his previous behaviour has been very suspicious.'

Entertainment

Throughout the first century A.D., the three theatres in Rome regularly provided popular entertainment at festival time. But there was a change in the kind of drama presented.

The traditional type of tragedy was losing its popularity and being replaced by pantomime. A pantomime had only one actor; he was known as a 'pantomīmus' (meaning 'acting everything') because he acted all the parts in the story, changing his mask as he changed characters. For example, a pantomimus who was presenting the love-affair of Mars and Venus would take the parts not only of Mars and Venus themselves but also of Helios the sun-god telling Venus' husband Vulcan about the affair, Vulcan setting a trap for the guilty pair, and the other gods coming one by one to look at Mars and Venus when they were caught in the act.

The pantomimus did not speak, but danced and mimed rather in the manner of a modern ballet dancer, and was often accompanied by an orchestra and a chorus who sang the words of the story. The

Model of the theatre of Pompey.

story itself was usually based on Greek myth but sometimes on history. The pantomimus represented the story's action with graceful movements and gestures; he needed plenty of physical skill and stamina, as well as an attractive appearance and a wide knowledge of literature. One of the most famous of all pantomimi was the dancer Paris, who appears in the stories of Stages 33 and 34.

In the same way that pantomimes were replacing tragedies, comedies were being replaced by mimes. A mime was a crude slapstick farce, usually on a theme taken from everyday life. The style of performance was generally obscene or grotesque or both.

The most popular form of public entertainment in Rome, however, was undoubtedly chariot-racing. Almost everybody, from the emperor downwards, took an interest in this sport. The Circus Maximus, where the most important chariot-racing took place, could hold 250,000 spectators – a far higher capacity than any modern football or baseball stadium. Much money changed hands in betting, and each of the rival chariot-teams was cheered on by its fans with passionate enthusiasm.

There were four teams (factiōnēs) competing regularly with each other: green, blue, red and white. Each team consisted of one, two or three chariots, and the commonest number of horses to a chariot was four. A day's programme normally consisted of twenty-four races, each lasting seven laps (about 8 kilometres or 5 miles) and taking about a quarter of an hour to run. Seven huge eggs of marble or wood were hoisted high above the central platform (spīna), and every time the chariots completed a lap, one egg was lowered. The charioteer had to race at full speed down the length of the circus and then display his greatest skill at the turning-point (mēta); if he took the bend too slowly he would be overtaken, and if he took it too fast he might crash. He raced with the reins tied tightly round his body, and in his belt he carried a knife; if he crashed, his life might depend on how quickly he could cut himself free from the wreckage.

Study the photograph and answer the questions that follow it.

1 How many charioteers are shown? Whereabouts in the circus are they?
2 What are the three objects placed on conical pillars on the right?
3 It has been suggested that the charioteer on the left is reining in the inside horse. Why would he do this?
4 The charioteer on the right seems to be whipping up his team. Why can he now drive them faster?

Another centre of entertainment was the Flavian amphitheatre, later known as the Colosseum. Up to 50,000 spectators could watch the gladiatorial combats and beast-hunts that took place here. On occasion, the arena was filled with water for the representation of sea battles.

Not all entertainment was public. Rich Romans enjoyed presenting private shows of various kinds, as in the story on pp. 87–9, where Paris performs in Haterius' garden for Vitellia and her friends. One elderly lady, Ummidia Quadratilla, kept her own private troupe of pantomimi. Often such entertainment would be presented at a dinner-party. This might consist of dancing-girls, freaks, actors, jugglers, acrobats, a band of musicians, a novelty like the philosopher Euphrosyne, or a trained slave reciting a poem or other literary work – possibly written by the host, which might sometimes be rather embarrassing for the guests. The more serious types of entertainment were often put on by highly educated hosts for equally cultivated and appreciative guests; but they might sometimes, like Euphrosyne's philosophy lecture, be presented by ignorant and uninterested hosts who merely wanted to be in the fashion or were trying to pass themselves off as persons of good taste and culture.

The Colosseum.

Words and phrases checklist

ācriter – keenly, fiercely
at – but
brevis, breve – short, brief
certō, certāre, certāvī – compete
coniciō, conicere, coniēcī, coniectus – hurl, throw
contrā – against, on the other hand
crās – tomorrow
ēiciō, ēicere, ēiēcī, ēiectus – throw out
et . . . et – both . . . and
excipiō, excipere, excēpī, exceptus – receive
fuga, fugae – escape
hīc – here
lēniter – gently
moveō, movēre, mōvī, mōtus – move
nisi – except, unless
obstupefaciō, obstupefacere, obstupefēcī, obstupefactus – amaze,
    stun
odiō sum, odiō esse – be hateful
potestās, potestātis – power
rēgīna, rēgīnae – queen
sevērus, sevēra, sevērum – severe, strict
tēctum, tēctī – ceiling, roof
utrum – whether

Numbers

ūnus – one	prīmus – first
duo – two	secundus – second
trēs – three	tertius – third
quattuor – four	quārtus – fourth
quīnque – five	quīntus – fifth
sex – six	sextus – sixth
septem – seven	septimus – seventh
octō – eight	octāvus – eighth
novem – nine	nōnus – ninth
decem – ten	decimus – tenth

vīgintī – twenty
trīgintā – thirty
quadrāgintā – forty
quīnquāgintā – fifty
sexāgintā – sixty
septuāgintā – seventy
octōgintā – eighty
nōnāgintā – ninety
centum – a hundred
ducentī – two hundred

lībertus

ultiō Epaphrodītī

Epaphrodītus, ā Paride atque Domitiā ēlūsus, eōs ulcīscī vehementissimē cupiēbat. Imperātor quoque, īrā et suspīciōne commōtus, Epaphrodītum saepe hortābātur ut Paridem Domitiamque pūnīret. Epaphrodītō tamen difficile erat Domitiam, uxōrem Imperātōris, et Paridem, pantomīmum nōtissimum, apertē accūsāre. auxilium igitur ab amīcō C. Salviō Līberāle petīvit.

Epaphrodītus 'nōn modo ego', inquit, 'sed etiam Imperātor poenās Paridis Domitiaeque cupit. sī mē in hāc rē adiūveris, magnum praemium tibi dabitur.'

Salvius, rē páulīsper cōgitātā, tranquillē respondit:

'cōnfīde mihi, amīce; ego tibi rem tōtam administrābō. īnsidiae parābuntur; Domitia et Paris in īnsidiās ēlicientur; ambō capientur et pūnientur.'

'quid Domitiae accidet?' rogāvit Epaphrodītus.

'Domitia accūsābitur; damnābitur; fortasse relēgābitur.'

'et Paris?'

Salvius rīsit.

'ēmovēbitur.'

ēlūsus: ēlūdere *trick, outwit*
ulcīscī *to take revenge on*
suspīciōne: suspīciō *suspicion*

ēlicientur: ēlicere *lure, entice*
relēgābitur: relēgāre *exile*

When you have read this story, answer the questions at the end.

īnsidiae

paucīs post diēbus Domitia ancillam, nōmine Chionēn, ad sē
vocāvit.
'epistulam', inquit, 'ā Vitelliā, uxōre Hateriī, missam modo
accēpī. ēheu! Vitellia in morbum gravem incidit. statim mihi
vīsitanda est. tē volō omnia parāre.'   5
    tum Chionē, e cubiculō dominae ēgressa, iussit lectīcam parārī et
lectīcāriōs arcessī. medicum quoque nōmine Asclēpiadēn quaesīvit
quī medicāmenta quaedam Vitelliae parāret. inde Domitia lectīcā
vecta, comitantibus servīs, domum Hateriī profecta est. difficile erat

Chionēn *Greek accusative of* Chionē   arcessī *to be summoned, to be sent for*
parārī *to be prepared*   Asclēpiadēn *Greek accusative of* Asclēpiadēs
lectīcāriōs: lectīcārius *chair-carrier,* medicāmenta: medicāmentum *medicine,*
  sedan-chair carrier   *drug*

eīs per viās prōgredī, quod nox obscūra erat multumque pluēbat. 10
cum domum Hateriī pervēnissent, iānuam apertam invēnērunt.
servīs extrā iānuam relictīs, Domitia cum Chionē ingressa est.
spectāculum inopīnātum eīs ingredientibus obiectum est. ātrium
magnificē ōrnātum erat: ubīque lūcēbant lucernae, corōnae
rosārum dē omnibus columnīs pendēbant. sed omnīnō dēsertum 15
erat ātrium. inde fēminae, triclīnium ingressae, id quoque dēsertum
vīdērunt. in mediō tamen cēna sūmptuōsa posita erat: mēnsae
epulīs exquīsītissimīs cumulātae erant, pōcula vīnō optimō plēna
erant. quibus vīsīs, ancilla timidā vōce,
    'cavendum est nōbīs', inquit. 'aliquid mīrī hīc agitur.' 20
    'fortasse Vitellia morbō affecta est cum cēnāret. sine dubiō iam in
cubiculō convalēscit', respondit Domitia, ignāra īnsidiārum quās
Salvius parāverat.
    itaque per domum dēsertam, ancillā timidē sequente, Domitia
prōgredī coepit. cum ad cubiculum ubi Vitellia dormīre solēbat 25
pervēnisset, in līmine cōnstitit. cubiculum erat obscūrum. Chionēn
ad triclīnium remīsit quae lucernam ferret. in silentiō noctis diū
exspectābat dum redīret ancilla. haec tamen nōn rediit. tandem
Domitia morae impatiēns in cubiculum irrūpit. vacuum erat. tum
dēmum pavōre magnō perturbāta est. tenebrae, silentium, ancillae 30
absentia, haec omnia perīculī indicia esse vidēbantur. scīlicet falsa
fuerat epistula, mendāx nūntius morbī!
    Domitia ad aulam quam celerrimē regredī cōnstituit priusquam
aliquid malī sibi accideret. dum per vacua conclāvia fugit, vōce
hominis subitō perterrita est. 35
    'dēliciae meae, salvē! tūne quoque ad cēnam invītāta es?'
    tum vōcem agnōvit.
    'mī Parī', inquit, 'īnsidiae, nōn cēna, nōbīs parātae sunt.
effugiendum nōbīs est, dum possumus.'

inopīnātum: inopīnātus *unexpected*	dum *until*
obiectum est *met, was presented*	vacuum: vacuus *empty*
epulīs: epulae *dishes*	tum dēmum *then at last, only then*
cumulātae erant: cumulāre *heap*	absentia *absence*
cavendum est: cavēre *beware*	vidēbantur: vidērī *seem*
mīrī: mīrus *extraordinary*	nūntius *message, news*
remīsit: remittere *send back*	

1 What message about Vitellia did Domitia receive? What did she decide to do immediately?
2 What preparations did Chione make?
3 Why was the journey difficult?
4 What did Domitia and Chione discover (*a*) at the entrance to the house (*b*) in the atrium (*c*) in the triclinium?
5 What explanation of the situation does Domitia give Chione in lines 21–2?
6 Where did Domitia and Chione go next? Why did Domitia send Chione back?
7 'haec tamen nōn rediit' (line 28). Suggest an explanation for this.
8 What did Domitia at last realise? What made her realise this?
9 Who is the speaker in line 36? How has he been lured to the house? Now that he and Domitia are at the house, what do you suppose will be the next step in Salvius' plan?

exitium

I

Domitiā haec dīcente, Myropnous, quī dominum comitābātur, ad iānuam contendit. cautē prōspexit. ecce! via tōta mīlitibus praetōriānīs plēna erat. neque lectīca, neque medicus, neque servī usquam vidērī poterant.

ad ātrium reversus Myropnous 'āctum est dē nōbīs!' exclāmāvit. 5
'appropinquant praetōriānī! mox hūc ingredientur!'

hōc tamen cognitō, Paris 'nōlī dēspērāre', inquit. 'cōnsilium habeō. Myropnū, tibi iānua custōdienda est. prohibē mīlitēs ingredī. sī mē vel Domitiam hōc locō cēperint, certē nōs interficient. cōnandum est nōbīs per postīcum ēlābī.' 1⃝

Myropnous igitur iānuam claudere contendit. quō factō ad triclīnium reversus lectōs mēnsāsque raptim in faucēs trahere coepit. sellās quoque ex ātriō, lectōs ē cubiculīs proximīs collēctōs in cumulum imposuit. brevī ingēns pyra in faucibus exstrūcta est.

mīlitēs praetōriānī, cum iānuam clausam cōnspexissent, 1⃝ haesitantēs cōnstitērunt. sed tribūnus, nē Paris et Domitia effugerent, iānuam effringī iussit. statim iānua secūribus pulsābātur. Myropnous ubi strepitum pulsantium audīvit pyram incendit. amphoram oleī ē culīnā portāvit quā flammās augēret. tum pyrā flagrante, amīcōs sequī contendit. 2⃝

praetōriānīs: praetōriānus *praetorian (member of emperor's bodyguard)*
usquam *anywhere*
reversus: revertī *return*
āctum est dē nōbīs *it's all over with us*
postīcum *back gate*
ēlābī *escape*
faucēs *passage, entrance-way*
imposuit: impōnere *put onto*
pyra *pyre*
secūribus: secūris *axe*
flagrante: flagrāre *blaze*

II

Paris et Domitia, ubi ad postīcum pervēnērunt, duōs mīlitēs ibi positōs invēnērunt. quōs cum vīdissent, quamquam Domitia omnīnō dē salūte dēspērābat, Paris in hōc discrīmine audācissimum atque callidissimum sē praestitit. nam cēlātā haud procul Domitiā, ipse per postīcum audācter prōgressus sē mīlitibus ostendit. tum 5
quasi fugiēns, retrō in hortum cucurrit.

    statim clāmāvērunt mīlitēs: 'ecce Paris! Paris effugere cōnātur!'

    mīlitibus sequentibus, Paris per hortum modo hūc modo illūc ruēbat. post statuās sē cēlābat mīlitēsque vōce blandā dērīdēbat. illī

retrō *back*   modo . . . modo *now . . . now*

incertī ubi esset pantomīmus, vōcem Paridis circā hortum 10
sequēbantur.

tandem audīvit Paris strepitum cēterōrum mīlitum domum
irrumpentium. brevī tōta domus mīlitibus plēna erat. tribūnus aliōs
iussit aquam ferre ut flammās exstinguerent, aliōs gladiīs dēstrictīs
omnēs domūs partēs perscrūtārī ut Paridem invenīrent. hic bene 15
intellēxit quantō in perīculō esset sed etiam tum haudquāquam
dēspērāvit.

mediō in hortō stābat laurus veterrima, quae tēctō domūs
imminēbat. simulatque intrāvērunt mīlitēs hortum, laurum Paris
cōnscendit. hinc prōsilīre in tēctum cōnātus est. prōsiluit, sed 20
tēgulae tēctī lūbricae erant. paulīsper in margine tēctī stetit; deinde
praeceps humum lāpsus est.

intereā Domitia, quae per postīcum nūllō vidente ēgressa erat,
haud procul exspectābat dum Paris ad sē venīret. lāpsō tamen
corpore eius, tantus erat fragor ut etiam ad aurēs Domitiae 25
advenīret. quae metū āmēns vītaeque suae neglegēns in hortum
reversa est. ubi corpus Paridis humī iacēns vīdit, dolōre cōnfecta sē
in eum coniēcit eīque ōscula multa dedit.

'valē, dēliciae meae, valē!'

adiit tribūnus. Domitiam ad aulam dēdūcī iussit. ipse caput 30
pantomīmī amputātum ad Epaphrodītum rettulit.

circā *around*	margine: margō *edge*
exstinguerent: exstinguere *put out*	nūllō *(used as ablative of* nēmō)*no one*
dēstrictīs: dēstringere *draw, unsheathe*	fragor *crash*
prōsilīre *jump*	āmēns *out of her mind, in a frenzy*
tēgulae: tēgula *tile*	cōnfecta: cōnfectus *overcome*
lūbricae: lūbricus *slippery*	amputātum: amputāre *cut off*

About the language

1   In Stage 13, you met sentences containing infinitives:

currere volō.   I want to run.
servī **labōrāre** nōn possunt.   The slaves are not able to work.

This kind of infinitive is known in full as the *present active infinitive*.

2 In Stage 34, you have met another kind of infinitive:

volō epistulam **recitārī**.   I want the letter to be read out.
Paris **invenīrī** nōn poterat. Paris was unable to be found.

This infinitive is known as the *present passive infinitive*.

3 Compare the following examples of present active and present
passive infinitives:

present active		*present passive*	
portāre	to carry	portārī	to be carried
docēre	to teach	docērī	to be taught
trahere	to drag	trahī	to be dragged
audīre	to hear	audīrī	to be heard

4 Further examples of the present passive infinitive:

1 volō iānuam aperīrī.
2 neque Vitellia neque ancilla vidērī poterant.
3 fūr capī nōlēbat.
4 dux iussit captīvum līberārī.

5 Notice how deponent verbs form their infinitive:

cōnārī	to try
pollicērī	to promise
ingredī	to enter
orīrī	to rise

Further examples:

1 lībertus iussit mīlitēs pantomīmum sequī.
2 aegrōtī deam precārī volēbant.
3 nūntius tandem proficīscī cōnstituit.
4 puerī tam perterritī erant ut loquī nōn possent.

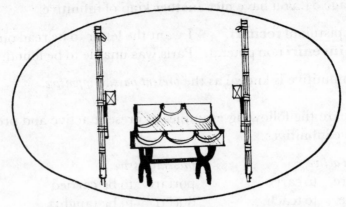

The consular chair and fasces which were the symbols of the consulship as promised to Salvius in the story. The *ornamenta praetoria* promised to Epaphroditus are discussed on page 123.

honōrēs

Salviō aulam intrantī obviam iit Epaphrodītus. cōmiter excēpit.

Epaphrodītus: mī Salvī, quālis artifex es! tuā arte iste pantomīmus occīsus est. tuā arte Domitia ex Ītaliā relēgāta est. Imperātor, summō gaudiō affectus, spectāculum splendidissimum in amphitheātrō Flāviō darī iussit. 5 crās diēs fēstus ab omnibus cīvibus celebrābitur; puerī puellaeque deōrum effigiēs corōnīs flōrum ōrnābunt; sacerdōtēs sacrificia offerent; ingēns cīvium multitūdō Imperātōrem ad templum Iovis comitābitur, ubi ille dīs immortālibus grātiās aget. 10 mox senātōrēs ad cūriam fēstīs vestīmentīs prōgredientur et Domitiānō grātulābuntur. venī mēcum! nōn morandum est nōbīs. Imperātor enim nōs exspectat. mihi ōrnāmenta praetōria, tibi cōnsulātum prōmīsit. 15

Salvius: cōnsulātum mihi prōmīsit? quam fortūnātus sum!

Epaphrodītus: venī! oportet nōs Imperātōrī grātiās agere.

Epaphrodītō et Salviō ēgressīs ut Domitiānum salūtārent, ē latebrīs
rēpsit Myropnous. manifesta nunc omnia erant. nunc dēnique
intellēxit quis esset auctor exitiī Paridis. lacrimīs effūsīs, indignam 20
amīcī mortem lūgēbat. tum manibus ad caelum sublātīs nōmen
Salviī dētestātus est. tībiās āmēns frēgit. ultiōnem sibi hīs verbīs
prōmīsit:
   'ego numquam iterum tībiīs cantābō priusquam pereat Salvius.'

artifex *artist*
cūriam: cūria *senate-house*
morandum est: morārī *delay*
ōrnāmenta praetōria *honorary praetorship, honorary rank of praetor*
manifesta: manifestus *clear*
auctor *person responsible*
indignam: indignus *unworthy, undeserved*
sublātīs: tollere *raise, lift up*
priusquam pereat *until . . . perishes*

About the language

1 Study the following examples:

crās nūntiī ad rēgem **mittentur**.
Tomorrow messengers will be sent to the king.

cēna sūmptuōsa ā servīs **parābitur**.
An expensive dinner will be prepared by the slaves.

The words in heavy print are passive forms of the future tense.

2 Compare the following active and passive forms:

future active	*future passive*
portābit	portābitur
he will carry	he will be carried
portābunt	portābuntur
they will carry	they will be carried
trahet	trahētur
he will drag	he will be dragged
trahent	trahentur
they will drag	they will be dragged

3 Further examples:

1 ingēns praemium victōrī dabitur.
2 omnēs vīllae dēlēbuntur.
3 Paris mox capiētur.
4 illī custōdēs quī in statiōne dormīvērunt sevērissimē pūnientur.

4 Notice how the future tense of deponent verbs is formed:

cōnābitur	he will try
cōnābuntur	they will try
loquētur	he will speak
loquentur	they will speak

Further examples:

1 mīlitēs crās proficīscentur.
2 dominus meus, quī stultissimus est, nihil suspicābitur.
3 multī senātōrēs Domitiānum ad forum comitābuntur.
4 sī inimīcus tuus hoc venēnum cōnsūmpserit, moriētur.

Practising the language

1 Study the form and meaning of the following verbs and nouns, and give the meaning of the untranslated words:

haesitāre	hesitate	haesitātiō	hesitation
nāvigāre	sail	nāvigātiō	voyage
coniūrāre	conspire	coniūrātiō	
mūtāre	change, alter	mūtātiō	
salūtāre		salūtātiō	
cōgitāre	think	cōgitātiō	
dubitāre		dubitātiō	

Match each of the following Latin nouns with the correct English translation:

Latin: rogātiō, festīnātiō, recūsātiō, hortātiō, recitātiō
English: haste, encouragement, request, refusal, public reading

2 Complete each sentence with the right word and then translate.

1 ego vōbīs rem tōtam . . . . . . (nārrābō, nārrābimus)
2 amīcī meī cibum vestīmentaque nōbīs . . . . . . (praebēbit, praebēbunt)
3 imperātor spectāculum splendidum in amphitheātrō crās . . . . . . (dabunt, dabit)
4 vōs estis fortiōrēs quam illī barbarī; eōs facile . . . . . (superābitis, superābis)
5 caudex! tū mē numquam . . . . . . (capiēs, capiētis)
6 tū in vīllā manē; nōs per postīcum . . . . . (effugiam, effugiēmus)
7 ego sum probus; ego tibi pecūniam . . . . . . (reddēmus, reddam)
8 fugite! hostēs mox . . . . . . (aderunt, aderit)

3 Translate each English sentence into Latin by selecting correctly from the list of Latin words.

1 Many flowers were being thrown by the spectators.

multa   flōris   ā spectātōribus   iactābant
multī   flōrēs   inter spectātōrēs   iactābantur

2 They warned my friend not to cross the bridge.

amīcum   meīs   monuerant   nē   pōns   trānsīret
amīcōs   meum   monuērunt   ut   pontem   trānsībat

3 Having been ordered by the leader, we carried out the body.

ad ducem   iussus   corpus   extulī
ā duce   iussī   corporum   extulimus

4 We saw the man whose brother you (*s.*) had arrested.

hominem   quī   frāter   comprehenderātis   vidēmus
hominum   cuius   frātrem   comprehenderās   vīdimus

5 When the soldiers had been drawn up (*two Latin words only*), I gave the centurion a sign.

mīlitibus   īnstrūctīs   centuriōnem   signum   dedī
mīlitēs   īnstrūctōs   centuriōnī   signō   dedit

4 In each pair of sentences, translate sentence 'a'; then, with the help of page 141 in the Language Information section, express the same idea in a different way by completing sentence 'b' with a passive form, and translate again.

For example: a   centuriō fūrēs vulnerāverat.
                b   fūrēs ā centuriōne . . . . . .

Translated and completed, this becomes:

a   centuriō fūrēs vulnerāverat.
    The centurion had wounded the thieves.

b   fūrēs ā centuriōne vulnerātī erant.
    The thieves had been wounded by the centurion.

The perfect and pluperfect tenses are both used in this exercise. The verbs in sentences 1–5 are all first conjugation like 'portō'.

1a   coquus cibum parāverat.
1b   cibus ā coquō . . . . . .
2a   mercātor latrōnēs superāverat.
2b   latrōnēs ā mercātōre . . . . . .

3a dominī servōs laudāvērunt.
3b servī ā dominīs . . . . . .
4a clientēs patrōnum salūtāvērunt.
4b patrōnus ā clientibus . . . . . .
5a rēx mē ipsum accūsāvit.
5b ego ipse ā rēge . . . . . .
6a custōs magnum clāmōrem audīvit.
6b magnus clāmor ā custōde . . . . . .

Freedmen

When a slave was set free (manumitted), he ceased to be the property of his master and became a 'lībertus' instead of a 'servus'. He also, as we have seen (p.61), became a 'cliēns' of his ex-master, and his ex-master was now his 'patrōnus'.

In addition, a freedman became a Roman citizen. He now had three names, of which the first two came from the name of his ex-master. (For example, Tiro, the freedman of Marcus Tullius Cicero, became Marcus Tullius Tiro.) As a citizen, he now had the right to vote in elections, and to make a will or business agreement which would be valid in the eyes of the law. He could also get married. If he had been living in an unofficial marriage with a slave-woman, one of his first acts after manumission might be to save up enough money to buy her out of slavery and marry her legally.

There were some limits to the rights and privileges of a freedman, compared with other Roman citizens. He could not become a senator or an 'eques', except by special favour of the emperor (and a freedwoman could not become a senator's wife). He could not serve in the legions, nor stand as a candidate in elections. One privilege, however, was available to freedmen and to no one else. A freedman could become one of the six priests (sēvirī Augustālēs) who were appointed in many Italian towns to look after the worship of the deified Emperor Augustus. Like all priesthoods, the priesthood of Augustus was a position of honour and prestige, and it was open to freedmen only.

Relief showing a manumission ceremony.

The law laid down certain obligations which a freedman owed to his ex-master. For example, a freedman was supposed to leave money to his ex-master in his will (ex-masters did not often insist on this); he was forbidden to do anything that would bring harm to his ex-master; and he had to do a certain number of days' work for his ex-master every year, or pay him a sum of money instead. It is clear from this that it would often be financially worthwhile for a master to manumit a slave; he would still be able to make some use of the ex-slave's services, but would no longer have to provide and pay for his food, clothing and shelter.

After manumission, a freedman had to put up with a certain amount of prejudice from those who despised him for having been a slave. He was also faced with the need to earn a living. His ex-master might help by providing money to start a small business, as Quintus did for Clemens in Stage 18, or introducing him to potential customers. Many highly skilled or educated freedmen were quickly able to earn a good living because they already possessed some special ability or experience; for example, a freedman might already be a skilled craftsman, teacher, musician or secretary, or be experienced in accountancy, trade or banking. Freedmen who had previously used these skills in their masters' service could now use them for their own benefit. There was plenty of demand for such services, and not much competition from freeborn Romans, who often lacked the necessary skills or regarded such work as below their dignity.

It is not surprising, therefore, that many freedmen became rich and successful, and a few freedmen became very rich indeed. The Vettii brothers, who set up their own business in Pompeii and eventually owned one of the most splendid houses in the town, are good examples of successful freedmen. But perhaps the most famous example of a wealthy freedman is a fictitious one: Trimalchio, the vulgar millionaire in Petronius' novel *Satyrica*. The story 'cēna Haterii' in Stage 32 is partly based on Petronius' account of Trimalchio's dinner-party.

Some freedmen continued to live in their ex-master's household, doing the same work that they had done as slaves. One such man was Pliny's talented freedman Zosimus, who was equally skilled at reciting, lyre-playing and comedy-acting. Pliny treated Zosimus with kindness and affection, and when Zosimus fell ill with tuberculosis, Pliny arranged a holiday abroad for him.

Further evidence of friendly relationships between ex-masters and freedmen comes from the large number of inscriptions, particularly on tombstones, that refer to freedmen and freedwomen. Sometimes, for example, freedmen set up tombstones in honour of their ex-masters:

D M

T. FLAVIO HOMERO T.

FLAVIVS HYACINTHVS

PATRONO BENE MERENTI

Sometimes ex-masters set up tombstones to their favourite freedmen:

D M

IVLIO VITALI

PATRONVS LIBERTO

BENE MERENTI

Some ex-masters allowed freedmen and freedwomen to be buried
with them in their tombs:

D M
TITVS FLAVIVS EV
MOLPVS ET FLAVIA
QVINTA SIBI FECE
RVNT ET LIBERTIS LI
BERTABVSQVE POS
TERISQVE EORVM

An ex-master might marry his freedwoman:

D M
T. FLAVIVS CERIALIS
FLAVIAE PHILAENIDI
LIBERTAE IDEM
ET COIVGI
B M F

A small but very important group of freedmen worked as personal
assistants to the emperor. As slaves, they had been known as 'servī
Caesaris', and as freedmen they were known as 'lībertī Augustī'.
('Caesar' and 'Augustus' were both used as titles of the emperor.)
One of these men was Epaphroditus, who worked first for Nero and
later for Domitian. He eventually fell out of favour with Domitian
and was executed in A.D.95 for having helped Nero to commit
suicide twenty-seven years earlier.

Epaphroditus' official title was secretary 'ā libellīs' ('in charge of
petitions' – the word 'ā' has an unusual meaning in this phrase),
which means that he helped the emperor to deal with the various
petitions or requests submitted to him by groups and individuals.
The opportunities for bribery are obvious. Other freedmen of the
emperor were in charge of correspondence (ab epistulīs) and
accounts (ā ratiōnibus). They all worked closely with the emperor
in the day-to-day running of government business.

Under some emperors, especially Claudius and Nero, these
freedmen became immensely rich and powerful. They were often
bitterly resented by the Roman nobles and senators. This

resentment can be seen very plainly in two letters which Pliny wrote about Pallas, the secretary 'ā ratiōnibus' of the Emperor Claudius. Pallas had been awarded the 'ōrnāmenta praetōria' (honorary praetorship), like Epaphroditus in the story on page 114. This means he was given the various privileges normally possessed by a praetor: special dress, special seat at public ceremonies, special funeral after death, and so on. Pliny, having come across the inscription commemorating these honours, is furiously angry. He describes Pallas as a 'furcifer', and much else besides. Even though the whole incident had happened fifty years previously, Pliny is boiling with indignation. He is particularly angry that the inscription praised Pallas for refusing a further gift of 15 million sesterces. In Pliny's opinion, Pallas was insulting the praetorian rank by refusing the money as excessive while accepting the privileges as if they meant less; besides he already had 300 million sesterces of his own. Pliny's outburst shows very clearly how much ill-feeling could be caused by an emperor's use of ex-slaves as important and powerful assistants in running the empire.

Words and phrases checklist

auctor, auctōris – creator, originator, person responsible
   mē auctōre – at my suggestion
cōnsulātus, cōnsulātūs – consulship (rank of consul)
damnō, damnāre, damnāvī, damnātus – condemn
dum – while, until
exstinguō, exstinguere, exstīnxī, exstīnctus – extinguish, put out, destroy
gaudium, gaudiī – joy
haud – not
immineō, imminēre, imminuī – hang over
impōnō, impōnere, imposuī, impositus – impose, put into, put onto
indicium, indiciī – sign, evidence

continued

lectīca, lectīcae – sedan-chair
modo – just
obviam eō, obviam īre, obviam iī – meet, go to meet
pendeō, pendēre, pependī – hang
priusquam – before, until
procul – far
quasi – as if
tenebrae, tenebrārum – darkness
ultiō, ultiōnis – revenge
vel – or
vestīmenta, vestīmentōrum – clothes

Deponent verbs

adipīscor, adipīscī, adeptus sum – obtain
amplector, amplectī, amplexus sum – embrace
comitor, comitārī, comitātus sum – accompany
cōnor, cōnārī, cōnātus sum – try
cōnspicor, cōnspicārī, cōnspicātus sum – catch sight of
ēgredior, ēgredī, ēgressus sum – go out
hortor, hortārī, hortātus sum – encourage, urge
ingredior, ingredī, ingressus sum – enter
loquor, loquī, locūtus sum – speak
morior, morī, mortuus sum – die
nāscor, nāscī, nātus sum – be born
patior, patī, passus sum – suffer
precor, precārī, precātus sum – pray (to)
proficīscor, proficīscī, profectus sum – set out
prōgredior, prōgredī, prōgressus sum – advance
regredior, regredī, regressus sum – go back, return
revertor, revertī, reversus sum – turn back, return
sequor, sequī, secūtus sum – follow
suspicor, suspicārī, suspicātus sum – suspect

Language
Information

Contents

PART ONE: About the language

Nouns

1	*first declension*	*second declension*			*third declension*
	f.	*m.*	*m.*	*n.*	*m.*
SINGULAR					
nominative and vocative	puella	servus (*voc.* serve)	puer	templum	mercātor
accusative	puellam	servum	puerum	templum	mercātōrem
genitive	puellae	servī	puerī	templī	mercātōris
dative	puellae	servō	puerō	templō	mercātōrī
ablative	puellā	servō	puerō	templō	mercātōre
PLURAL					
nominative and vocative	puellae	servī	puerī	templa	mercātōrēs
accusative	puellās	servōs	puerōs	templa	mercātōrēs
genitive	puellārum	servōrum	puerōrum	templōrum	mercātōrum
dative	puellīs	servīs	puerīs	templīs	mercātōribus
ablative	puellīs	servīs	puerīs	templīs	mercātōribus

	fourth declension		*fifth declension*
	f.	*n.*	*m.*
SINGULAR			
nominative and vocative	manus	genū	diēs
accusative	manum	genū	diem
genitive	manūs	genūs	diēī
dative	manuī	genū	diēī
ablative	manū	genū	diē
PLURAL			
nominative and vocative	manūs	genua	diēs
accusative	manūs	genua	diēs
genitive	manuum	genuum	diērum
dative	manibus	genibus	diēbus
ablative	manibus	genibus	diēbus

m.	*m.*	*m.*	*f.*	*n.*	*n.*	
						SINGULAR
leō	cīvis	rēx	urbs	nōmen	tempus	*nominative and vocative*
leōnem	cīvem	rēgem	urbem	nōmen	tempus	*accusative*
leōnis	cīvis	rēgis	urbis	nōminis	temporis	*genitive*
leōnī	cīvī	rēgī	urbī	nōminī	temporī	*dative*
leōne	cīve	rēge	urbe	nōmine	tempore	*ablative*
						PLURAL
leōnēs	cīvēs	rēgēs	urbēs	nōmina	tempora	*nominative and vocative*
leōnēs	cīvēs	rēgēs	urbēs	nōmina	tempora	*accusative*
leōnum	cīvium	rēgum	urbium	nōminum	temporum	*genitive*
leōnibus	cīvibus	rēgibus	urbibus	nōminibus	temporibus	*dative*
leōnibus	cīvibus	rēgibus	urbibus	nōminibus	temporibus	*ablative*

2   For the ways in which the different cases are used, see pp. 148–49.

3   You have now met all the declensions and all the cases.

4   Notice again the way in which the cases of third declension nouns are formed. In particular, compare the nominative singular of 'leō', 'rēx' and 'nōmen' with the genitive singular and other cases. Use the list on pp. 156–181 to find the genitive singular of the following nouns, and then use the table above to find their ablative singular and plural:

dux; homō; pēs; difficultās; nox; iter.

Adjectives

1 first and second declension:

	masculine	feminine	neuter	masculine	feminine	neuter
SINGULAR						
nominative and vocative	bonus (*voc.* bone)	bona	bonum	pulcher	pulchra	pulchrum
accusative	bonum	bonam	bonum	pulchrum	pulchram	pulchrum
genitive	bonī	bonae	bonī	pulchrī	pulchrae	pulchrī
dative	bonō	bonae	bonō	pulchrō	pulchrae	pulchrō
ablative	bonō	bonā	bonō	pulchrō	pulchrā	pulchrō
PLURAL						
nominative and vocative	bonī	bonae	bona	pulchrī	pulchrae	pulchra
accusative	bonōs	bonās	bona	pulchrōs	pulchrās	pulchra
genitive	bonōrum	bonārum	bonōrum	pulchrōrum	pulchrārum	pulchrōru
dative		bonīs			pulchrīs	
ablative		bonīs			pulchrīs	

2 third declension:

	masc. and fem.	neuter	masc. and fem.	neuter
SINGULAR				
nominative and vocative	fortis	forte	ingēns	ingēns
accusative	fortem	forte	ingentem	ingēns
genitive	fortis		ingentis	
dative	fortī		ingentī	
ablative	fortī		ingentī	
PLURAL				
nominative and vocative	fortēs	fortia	ingentēs	ingentia
accusative	fortēs	fortia	ingentēs	ingentia
genitive	fortium		ingentium	
dative	fortibus		ingentibus	
ablative	fortibus		ingentibus	

3 Compare the third declension adjectives in paragraph 2 with the third declension nouns on pp. 128–29. Notice in particular the different form of the ablative singular.

4 With the help of paragraphs 1 and 2 opposite and the table of nouns on pp. 128–29, find the Latin for the words in italics in the following sentences:

1 I took the *brave girl* to the centurion.
2 He was the son of a *good king*.
3 They were attacked by a *huge slave*. (ablative)
4 We visited many *beautiful cities*.
5 The robbers were driven off by the *brave merchant*. (ablative)
6 The walls of the *huge temples* were built slowly and carefully.

Comparison of adjectives

1

	comparative	*superlative*
longus	longior	longissimus
long	*longer*	*longest, very long*
pulcher	pulchrior	pulcherrimus
beautiful	*more beautiful*	*most beautiful, very beautiful*
fortis	fortior	fortissimus
brave	*braver*	*bravest, very brave*
fēlīx	fēlīcior	fēlīcissimus
lucky	*luckier*	*luckiest, very lucky*
prūdēns	prūdentior	prūdentissimus
shrewd	*shrewder*	*shrewdest, very shrewd*
facilis	facilior	facillimus
easy	*easier*	*easiest, very easy*

2 Irregular forms:

bonus	melior	optimus
good	*better*	*best, very good*
malus	peior	pessimus
bad	*worse*	*worst, very bad*
magnus	maior	maximus
big	*bigger*	*biggest, very big*
parvus	minor	minimus
small	*smaller*	*smallest, very small*
multus	plūs	plūrimus
much	*more*	*most, very much*
multī	plūrēs	plūrimī
many	*more*	*most, very many*

3 Study the forms of the comparative adjective 'longior' ('longer') and the superlative adjective 'longissimus' ('longest, very long'):

	masc. and fem.	*neuter*	*masculine*	*feminine*	*neuter*
SINGULAR					
nominative and vocative	longior	longius	longissimus (*voc.*longissime)	longissima	longissimum
accusative	longiōrem	longius	longissimum	longissimam	longissimum
genitive	longiōris		longissimī	longissimae	longissimī
dative	longiōrī		longissimō	longissimae	longissimō
ablative	longiōre		longissimō	longissimā	longissimō
PLURAL					
nominative and vocative	longiōrēs	longiōra	longissimī	longissimae	longissima
accusative	longiōrēs	longiōra	longissimōs	longissimās	longissima
genitive	longiōrum		longissimōrum	longissimārum	longissimōrum
dative	longiōribus			longissimīs	
ablative	longiōribus			longissimīs	

4 Compare the endings of 'longior' with those of the third declension nouns 'mercātor' and 'tempus' on pp. 128 and 129. Notice in particular the nominative and accusative forms of the neuter singular.

5 With the help of paragraphs 1–3 and the table of nouns on pp. 4–5, find the Latin for the words in italics in the following sentences:

1 I have never known a *shrewder merchant*.

2 She sent the *worst slaves* back to the slave-dealer.

3 *Better times* will come.

4 The *bravest citizens* were fighting in the front line.

5 We did not visit the *biggest temple*, as we had seen a *more beautiful temple* next to it.

Pronouns

1   ego and tū ('I', 'you', etc.)

	singular		plural	
nominative	ego	tū	nōs	vōs
accusative	mē	tē	nōs	vōs
genitive	meī	tuī	nostrum	vestrum
dative	mihi	tibi	nōbīs	vōbīs
ablative	mē	tē	nōbīs	vōbīs

2   sē ('himself', 'herself', 'themselves', etc.)

	singular	plural
accusative	sē	sē
genitive	suī	suī
dative	sibi	sibi
ablative	sē	sē

3   hic ('this', 'these', etc.)

	singular			plural		
	masculine	*feminine*	*neuter*	*masculine*	*feminine*	*neuter*
nominative	hic	haec	hoc	hī	hae	haec
accusative	hunc	hanc	hoc	hōs	hās	haec
genitive		huius		hōrum	hārum	hōrum
dative		huic			hīs	
ablative	hōc	hāc	hōc		hīs	

The various forms of 'hic' can also be used to mean 'he', 'she', 'they', etc.:

hic tamen nihil dīcere poterat.
He, however, could say nothing.

4 ille ('that', 'those', etc.; sometimes used with the meaning 'he', 'she', 'it', etc.)

	singular			*plural*		
	masculine	*feminine*	*neuter*	*masculine*	*feminine*	*neuter*
nominative	ille	illa	illud	illī	illae	illa
accusative	illum	illam	illud	illōs	illās	illa
genitive		illīus		illōrum	illārum	illōrum
dative		illī			illīs	
ablative	illō	illā	illō		illīs	

5 ipse ('myself', 'yourself', 'himself', etc.)

	singular			*plural*		
	masculine	*feminine*	*neuter*	*masculine*	*feminine*	*neuter*
nominative	ipse	ipsa	ipsum	ipsī	ipsae	ipsa
accusative	ipsum	ipsam	ipsum	ipsōs	ipsās	ipsa
genitive		ipsīus		ipsōrum	ipsārum	ipsōrum
dative		ipsī			ipsīs	
ablative	ipsō	ipsā	ipsō		ipsīs	

6 **is** ('he', 'she', 'it', etc.)

	singular			plural		
	masculine	*feminine*	*neuter*	*masculine*	*feminine*	*neuter*
nominative	is	ea	id	eī	eae	ea
accusative	eum	eam	id	eōs	eās	ea
genitive		eius		eōrum	eārum	eōrum
dative		eī			eīs	
ablative	eō	eā	eō		eīs	

The forms of 'is' can also be used to mean 'that', 'those', etc.:

eā nocte rediit dominus.   That night, the master returned.

7 From Stage 23 onwards, you have met various forms of the word **īdem**, meaning 'the same':

	singular			plural		
	masculine	*feminine*	*neuter*	*masculine*	*feminine*	*neuter*
nominative	īdem	eadem	idem	eīdem	eaedem	eadem
accusative	eundem	eandem	idem	eōsdem	eāsdem	eadem
genitive		eiusdem		eōrundem	eārundem	eōrundem
dative		eīdem			eīsdem	
ablative	eōdem	eādem	eōdem		eīsdem	

Compare the forms of 'īdem' with 'is' in paragraph 6.

With the help of the table above, find the Latin for the words in italics in the following sentences:

1 I heard *the same* boy again.   3 This is *the same* man's house.
2 *The same* women were there.   4 He saw *the same* girl.

8 Notice the genitive, dative and ablative plural of the relative pronoun **quī**:

	singular			plural		
	masculine	*feminine*	*neuter*	*masculine*	*feminine*	*neuter*
nominative	quī	quae	quod	quī	quae	quae
accusative	quem	quam	quod	quōs	quās	quae
genitive		cuius		quōrum	quārum	quōrum
dative		cui			quibus	
ablative	quō	quā	quō		quibus	

duōs servōs ēmī, quōrum alter Graecus, alter Aegyptius erat.
I bought two slaves, one of whom was a Greek, the other an
Egyptian.

nūntiī quibus mandāta dedimus heri discessērunt.
The messengers to whom we gave the instructions departed
yesterday.

9 Notice again the use of the *connecting relative* to begin a sentence:

mīles pecūniam custōdiēbat. quem cum cōnspexissent, fūrēs
fūgērunt.
A soldier was guarding the money. When they caught sight of
him, the thieves ran away.

centuriō 'ad carnificēs dūcite!' inquit. quibus verbīs perterritī,
captīvī clāmāre ac lacrimāre coepērunt.
'Take them to the executioners!' said the centurion. Terrified by
these words, the prisoners began to shout and weep.

10 Sometimes the relative pronoun is used with forms of the
pronoun 'is':

fēcī **id** quod iussistī.
I have done *that* which you ordered.

Or, in more natural English, using the word 'what' ͵to translate
both Latin words:

fēcī **id quod** iussistī.
I have done *what* you ordered.

Further examples:

1 id quod Salvius in epistulā scrīpsit falsum est.
2 nūntius ea patefēcit quae apud Britannōs audīverat.
3 id quod mihi dīxistī vix intellegere possum.
4 servus tamen, homō ignāvissimus, id quod dominus iusserat
  omnīnō neglēxit.

Verbs

Indicative active

1

first conjugation	*second conjugation*	*third conjugation*	*fourth conjugation*
PRESENT *('I carry', etc.)*			
portō	doceō	trahō	audiō
portās	docēs	trahis	audīs
portat	docet	trahit	audit
portāmus	docēmus	trahimus	audīmus
portātis	docētis	trahitis	audītis
portant	docent	trahunt	audiunt
IMPERFECT *('I was carrying', etc.)*			
portābam	docēbam	trahēbam	audiēbam
portābās	docēbās	trahēbās	audiēbās
portābat	*etc.*	*etc.*	*etc.*
portābāmus			
portābātis			
portābant			

2 In Stage 33, you met the FUTURE tense (*'I shall carry'*, etc.):

portābō	docēbō	traham	audiam
portābis	docēbis	trahēs	audiēs
portābit	*etc.*	trahet	*etc.*
portābimus		trahēmus	
portābitis		trahētis	
portābunt		trahent	

Notice again how the first and second conjugations form their future tense in one way, the third and fourth conjugations in another.

3 In paragraph 2, find the Latin for:

they will carry; we shall drag; you (s.) will teach; I shall hear; you (pl.) will drag; he will carry.

What would be the Latin for the following?

he will teach; we shall hear; they will hear; you (pl.) will teach.

4 Translate each word, then with the help of paragraph 2 change it into the future tense, keeping the same person and number (i.e. 1st person singular, etc.), and translate again. For example, 'portāmus' ('we carry') would become 'portābimus' ('we shall carry'):

portātis; docēbam; docēbāmus; trahō; audīs; audiēbat.

5

first conjugation	*second conjugation*	*third conjugation*	*fourth conjugation*
PERFECT *('I have carried', 'I carried', etc.)*			
portāvī	docuī	trāxī	audīvī
portāvistī	docuistī	trāxistī	audīvistī
portāvit	*etc.*	*etc.*	*etc.*
portāvimus			
portāvistis			
portāvērunt			
PLUPERFECT *('I had carried', etc.)*			
portāveram	docueram	trāxeram	audīveram
portāverās	docuerās	trāxerās	audīverās
portāverat	*etc.*	*etc.*	*etc.*
portāverāmus			
portāverātis			
portāverant			

6 In Stage 33, you met the FUTURE PERFECT tense:

portāverō	docuerō	trāxerō	audīverō
portāveris	docueris	trāxeris	audīveris
portāverit	*etc.*	*etc.*	*etc.*
portāverimus			
portāveritis			
portāverint			

The future perfect is often translated by an English present tense:

sī effūgerō, iter ad vōs faciam.
If I escape, I shall make my way to you.

7 For passive and other forms of the verb, see pp. 140–43.

Indicative passive

1 In Stage 29, you met the following forms of the *passive*:

first conjugation	*second conjugation*	*third conjugation*	*fourth conjugation*
PRESENT			
portātur *he is (being) carried*	docētur *he is (being) taught*	trahitur *he is (being) dragged*	audītur *he is (being) heard*
portantur *they are (being) carried*	docentur *they are (being) taught*	trahuntur *they are (being) dragged*	audiuntur *they are (being) heard*
IMPERFECT			
portābātur *he was being carried*	docēbātur *he was being taught*	trahēbātur *he was being dragged*	audiēbātur *he was being heard*
portābantur *they were being carried*	docēbantur *they were being taught*	trahēbantur *they were being dragged*	audiēbantur *they were being heard*

2 Translate each word, then change it from singular to plural, so that it means 'they . . .' instead of 'he . . .' or 'it . . .', and translate again:

audītur; trahēbātur; dūcēbātur; laudātur; custōdiēbātur; dēlētur.

3 Forms of the FUTURE passive are given on page 116, Stage 34.

4 In Stage 30, you met the PERFECT and PLUPERFECT tenses of the passive:

first *conjugation*	*second* *conjugation*	*third* *conjugation*	*fourth* *conjugation*
PERFECT (*'I have been carried'*, *'I was carried'*, *etc.*)			
portātus sum	doctus sum	tractus sum	audītus sum
portātus es	doctus es	tractus es	audītus es
portātus est	*etc.*	*etc.*	*etc.*
portātī sumus			
portātī estis			
portātī sunt			
PLUPERFECT (*'I had been carried'*, *etc.*)			
portātus eram	doctus eram	tractus eram	audītus eram
portātus erās	doctus erās	tractus erās	audītus erās
portātus erat	*etc.*	*etc.*	*etc.*
portātī erāmus			
portātī erātis			
portātī erant			

5 Give the meaning of:

audītus eram; portātus erat; portātī sunt; doctus sum; tractus es; portātī erāmus.

6 In paragraph 4, find the Latin for:

they had been carried; I have been dragged; you (s.) have been taught; he was carried.

What would be the Latin for the following?

he has been taught; he had been dragged; we have been heard; they were heard.

7 Notice again that the two tenses in paragraph 4 are formed with perfect passive participles, which change their endings to indicate *number* (singular and plural) and *gender* (masculine, feminine and neuter). For example:

masculine singular:	puer ā mīlitibus **captus** est.
neuter singular:	templum ā mīlitibus **captum** est.
feminine singular:	urbs ā mīlitibus **capta** est.
feminine plural:	multae urbēs ā mīlitibus **captae** sunt.

8 For subjunctive and other forms of the verb, see pp. 142–43.

Subjunctive forms

1

first *conjugation*	*second* *conjugation*	*third* *conjugation*	*fourth* *conjugation*
IMPERFECT SUBJUNCTIVE			
portārem	docērem	traherem	audīrem
portārēs	docērēs	traherēs	audīrēs
portāret	*etc.*	*etc.*	*etc.*
portārēmus			
portārētis			
portārent			
PLUPERFECT SUBJUNCTIVE			
portāvissem	docuissem	trāxissem	audīvissem
portāvissēs	docuissēs	trāxissēs	audīvissēs
portāvisset	*etc.*	*etc.*	*etc.*
portāvissēmus			
portāvissētis			
portāvissent			

2   For ways in which the subjunctive is used see pp. 152–53.

Other forms of the verb

1   INFINITIVE

portāre	docēre	trahere	audīre
to carry	*to teach*	*to drag*	*to hear*

The form of the *passive* infinitive of each conjugation is given on page 113, Stage 34.

2   IMPERATIVE SINGULAR AND PLURAL

portā, portāte	docē, docēte	trahe, trahite	audī, audīte
carry!	*teach!*	*drag!*	*hear!*

3   PRESENT PARTICIPLE

portāns	docēns	trahēns	audiēns
carrying	*teaching*	*dragging*	*hearing*

Study the forms of the present participle 'portāns':

	singular		plural	
	masc. and fem.	neuter	masc. and fem.	neuter
nominative and vocative	portāns	portāns	portantēs	portantia
accusative	portantem	portāns	portantēs	portantia
genitive	portantis		portantium	
dative	portantī		portantibus	
ablative	portantī		portantibus	

The ablative singular of present participles sometimes ends in '-e', e.g. 'portante', 'docente'.

4 PERFECT PASSIVE PARTICIPLE

first conjugation	second conjugation	third conjugation	fourth conjugation
portātus *having been carried*	doctus *having been taught*	tractus *having been dragged*	audītus *having been heard*

Perfect passive participles change their endings in the same way as 'bonus' (shown on p. 130).

For examples of perfect *active* participles, see Deponent verbs, p. 144.

For examples of ways in which participles are used, see pp. 150–51.

5 FUTURE PARTICIPLE

portātūrus *about to carry*	doctūrus *about to teach*	tractūrus *about to drag*	audītūrus *about to hear*

Future participles change their endings in the same way as 'bonus'.

6 GERUNDIVE

portandus	docendus	trahendus	audiendus

Gerundives change their endings in the same way as 'bonus'.

Notice again the way in which the gerundive is used:

nōbīs audiendum est.   mihi amphora portanda est.
We must listen.   I must carry the wine-jar.

Deponent verbs

1 From Stage 32 onwards, you have met *deponent verbs*:

PRESENT			
cōnātur	*he tries*	loquitur	*he speaks*
cōnantur	*they try*	loquuntur	*they speak*

IMPERFECT			
cōnābātur	*he was trying*	loquēbātur	*he was speaking*
cōnābantur	*they were trying*	loquēbantur	*they were speaking*

PERFECT			
cōnātus sum	*I (have) tried*	locūtus sum	*I spoke, I have spoken*
cōnātus es	*you (have) tried*	locūtus es	*you spoke, you have spoken*
cōnātus est	*he (has) tried*	locūtus est	*he spoke, he has spoken*
cōnātī sumus	*we (have) tried*	locūtī sumus	*we spoke, we have spoken*
cōnātī estis	*you (have) tried*	locūtī estis	*you spoke, you have spoken*
cōnātī sunt	*they (have) tried*	locūtī sunt	*they spoke, they have spoken*

PLUPERFECT			
cōnātus eram	*I had tried*	locūtus eram	*I had spoken*
cōnātus erās	*you had tried*	locūtus erās	*you had spoken*
cōnātus erat	*he had tried*	locūtus erat	*he had spoken*
cōnātī erāmus	*we had tried*	locūtī erāmus	*we had spoken*
cōnātī erātis	*you had tried*	locūtī erātis	*you had spoken*
cōnātī erant	*they had tried*	locūtī erant	*they had spoken*

PERFECT ACTIVE PARTICIPLE			
cōnātus	*having tried*	locūtus	*having spoken*

Perfect active participles change their endings in the same way as 'bonus' (shown on p. 130).

INFINITIVE			
cōnārī	*to try*	loquī	*to speak*

Forms of the FUTURE tense of deponent verbs are given on p. 116, Stage 34.

2 The present and imperfect tenses are shown only in the form of the 3rd person singular and plural. You have not yet met the 1st and 2nd persons ('I try', 'you try', etc.) in the stories in the Stages.

3 Give the meaning of:

cōnātus eram; locūtī sumus; ingressī sumus; ingressus erās; profectus es.

4 Translate each word (or pair of words), then change it from plural to singular, so that it means 'he . . .' instead of 'they . . .', and translate again.

loquuntur; cōnātī sunt; profectī sunt; sequēbantur; ēgressī erant; hortantur.

5 Compare the two verbs in paragraph 1 with the passive forms of 'portō' and 'trahō' listed on pp. 140–41 above.

6 For further practice of deponent verbs, see paragraphs 4–5 on p. 155.

Irregular verbs

1

INFINITIVE					
esse	posse	īre	velle	ferre	capere
to be	*to be able*	*to go*	*to want*	*to bring*	*to take*

PRESENT (INDICATIVE) *('I am', etc.)*

sum	possum	eō	volō	ferō	capiō
es	potes	īs	vīs	fers	capis
est	potest	it	vult	fert	capit
sumus	possumus	īmus	volumus	ferimus	capimus
estis	potestis	ītis	vultis	fertis	capitis
sunt	possunt	eunt	volunt	ferunt	capiunt

IMPERFECT (INDICATIVE) *('I was', etc.)*

eram	poteram	ībam	volēbam	ferēbam	capiēbam
erās	poterās	ībās	volēbās	ferēbās	capiēbās
erat	*etc.*	*etc.*	*etc.*	*etc.*	*etc.*
erāmus					
erātis					
erant					

2 Study the forms of the FUTURE tense *('I shall be', etc.)*:

erō	poterō	ībō	volam	feram	capiam
eris	poteris	ībis	volēs	ferēs	capiēs
erit	poterit	ībit	volet	feret	capiet
erimus	poterimus	ībimus	*etc.*	*etc.*	*etc.*
eritis	poteritis	ībitis			
erunt	poterunt	ībunt			

3 Translate each word, then change it into the future tense, keeping the same person and number (i.e. 1st person singular, etc.), and translate again:

est; potestis; ībam; vīs; ferunt; capiēbāmus.

4 PERFECT (INDICATIVE) *('I have been', etc.)*

fuī	potuī	iī	voluī	tulī	cēpī
fuistī	potuistī	iistī	voluistī	tulistī	cēpistī
etc.	*etc.*	*etc.*	*etc.*	*etc.*	*etc.*

PLUPERFECT (INDICATIVE) *('I had been', etc.)*

fueram	potueram	ieram	volueram	tuleram	cēperam
fuerās	potuerās	ierās	voluerās	tulerās	cēperās
etc.	*etc.*	*etc.*	*etc.*	*etc.*	*etc.*

5 IMPERFECT SUBJUNCTIVE

essem	possem	īrem	vellem	ferrem	caperem
essēs	possēs	īrēs	vellēs	ferrēs	caperēs
etc.	*etc.*	*etc.*	*etc.*	*etc.*	*etc.*

PLUPERFECT SUBJUNCTIVE

fuissem	potuissem	iissem	voluissem	tulissem	cēpissem
fuissēs	potuissēs	iissēs	voluissēs	tulissēs	cēpissēs
etc.	*etc.*	*etc.*	*etc.*	*etc.*	*etc.*

6 For passive forms of 'ferō' and 'capiō', see p. 148.

7   Study the following *passive* forms of 'ferō' and 'capiō':

PRESENT			
fertur	*he is brought*	capitur	*he is taken*
feruntur	*they are brought*	capiuntur	*they are taken*

IMPERFECT			
ferēbātur	*he was being brought*	capiēbātur	*he was being taken*
ferēbantur	*they were being brought*	capiēbantur	*they were being taken*

PERFECT			
lātus sum	*I have been brought, I was brought*	captus sum	*I have been taken, I was taken*
lātus es	*you have been brought, you were brought*	captus es	*you have been taken, you were taken*
etc.		*etc.*	

PLUPERFECT			
lātus eram	*I had been brought*	captus eram	*I had been taken*
lātus erās	*you had been brought*	captus erās	*you had been taken*
etc.		*etc.*	

PERFECT PASSIVE PARTICIPLE			
lātus	*having been brought*	captus	*having been taken*

8   Give the meaning of:

captus erat; lātī erant; lātī sunt; captī sumus.

What would be the Latin for the following?

he had been brought; he has been taken; we have been brought; they were taken.

Uses of the cases

1 *nominative*
captīvus clāmābat.   The prisoner was shouting.

2 *vocative*
valē, **domine**!   Goodbye, master!

3 *accusative*

3a **pontem** trānsiimus.	We crossed the bridge.
3b **trēs hōrās** labōrābam.	I was working for three hours. (Compare 6d)
3c per **agrōs**; ad **vīllam**	through the fields; to the house (Compare 6e)

4 *genitive*

4a māter **puerōrum**	the mother of the boys
4b plūs **pecūniae**	more money
4c vir **maximae virtūtis**	a man of very great courage

5 *dative*

5a **mīlitibus** cibum dedimus.	We gave food to the soldiers.
5b **vestrō candidātō** nōn faveō.	I do not support your candidate.

6 *ablative*

6a **spectāculō** attonitus	astonished by the sight
6b senex **longā barbā**	an old man with a long beard
6c **nōbilī gente** nātus	born from a noble family
6d **quārtō diē** revēnit.	He came back on the fourth day. (Compare 3b)
6e cum **amīcīs**; ē **tabernā**	with friends; from the inn (Compare 3c)

For examples of 'ablative absolute' phrases, see paragraph 4 on p. 151.

7 Further examples of some of the uses listed above:

1 Vitellia erat fēmina summae prūdentiae.
2 sextā hōrā discessimus.
3 uxor imperātōris in ātriō aulae sedēbat.
4 Haterius, verbīs Salviī dēceptus, cōnsēnsit.
5 multōs annōs ibi habitābam.
6 cūr cōnsiliīs meīs obstās?
7 satis vīnī bibistī?

Uses of the participle

1   In Unit IIIA you saw how a participle changes its endings to agree with the noun it describes.

2   Translate the following examples and pick out the participle in each sentence:

1 ingēns multitūdō lūdōs, ab imperātōre ēditōs, spectābat.
2 custōdēs captīvō dormientī appropinquāvērunt.
3 mīlitēs, ā centuriōnibus īnstrūctī, in longīs ōrdinibus stābant.
4 mercātor amīcum, ā Graeciā regressum, ad cēnam sūmptuōsam invītāvit.

Find the nouns described by the participles in the sentences above, and say whether each noun-and-participle pair is nominative, accusative or dative.

3   Notice again some of the various ways in which a participle can be translated:

fūrēs, canem cōnspicātī, fūgērunt.
The thieves, having caught sight of the dog, ran away.
When the thieves caught sight of the dog, they ran away.
On catching sight of the dog, the thieves ran away.
The thieves ran away because they had caught sight of the dog.

4 In Stage 31, you met examples of *ablative absolute* phrases, consisting of a noun and participle in the ablative case:

bellō cōnfectō, Agricola ad Ītaliam rediit.
With the war having been finished, Agricola returned to Italy.
   Or, in more natural English:
When the war had been finished, Agricola returned to Italy, *or*
After finishing the war, Agricola returned to Italy.

Further examples:

1 ponte dēlētō, nēmō flūmen trānsīre poterat.
2 hīs verbīs audītīs, cīvēs plausērunt.
3 nāve refectā, mercātor ā Britanniā discessit.
4 iuvenēs, togīs dēpositīs, balneum intrāvērunt.
5 cōnsule ingressō, omnēs senātōrēs surrēxērunt.
6 fēle absente, mūrēs semper lūdunt.

5 From Stage 31 onwards, you have met examples in which a noun and participle in the *dative* case are placed at the beginning of the sentence:

amīcō auxilium petentī multam pecūniam obtulī.
To a friend asking for help I offered a lot of money.
   Or, in more natural English:
When my friend asked for help I offered him a lot of money.

Further examples:

1 servō haesitantī Vitellia 'intrā!' inquit.
2 Hateriō haec rogantī Salvius nihil respondit.
3 praecōnī regressō senex epistulam trādidit.
4 puellae prōcēdentī obstābat ingēns multitūdō clientium.

Uses of the subjunctive

1 *with 'cum' (meaning 'when')*

Iūdaeī, cum cōnsilium Eleazārī audīvissent, libenter cōnsēnsērunt.
When the Jews had heard Eleazar's plan, they willingly agreed.

2 *indirect question*

cōnsul nesciēbat quis arcum novum aedificāvisset.
The consul did not know who had built the new arch.

mē rogāvērunt num satis pecūniae habērem.
They asked me whether I had enough money.

From Stage 28 onwards, you have met the words 'utrum' and 'an' in indirect questions:

incertī erant utrum dux mortuus an vīvus esset.
They were unsure whether their leader was dead or alive.

3 *purpose clause*

ad urbem iter fēcimus ut amphitheātrum vīsitārēmus.
We travelled to the city in order to visit the amphitheatre.

In Stage 29, you met purpose clauses used with the relative pronoun 'quī':

nūntiōs ēmīsit quī prīncipēs ad aulam arcesserent.
He sent out messengers who were to summon the chieftains to the palace.
    Or, in more natural English:
He sent out messengers to summon the chieftains to the palace.

From Stage 29 onwards, you have met purpose clauses used with 'nē':

centuriō omnēs portās clausit nē captīvī effugerent.
The centurion shut all the gates so that the prisoners should not escápe.

4 *indirect command*

Domitiānus Salviō imperāverat ut rēgnum Cogidubnī occupāret.
Domitian had ordered Salvius to seize Cogidubnus' kingdom.

In Stage 29, you met indirect commands introduced by 'nē':

puella agricolam ōrāvit nē equum occīderet.
The girl begged the farmer not to kill the horse.

Haterius ab amīcīs monitus est nē Salviō cōnfīderet.
Haterius was warned by friends not to trust Salvius.

5 *result clause*

tam perītus erat tībīcen ut omnēs eum laudārent.
The piper was so skilful that everyone praised him.

6 Translate the following examples:

1 cum servī vīnum intulissent, Haterius silentium poposcit.
2 tanta erat fortitūdō Iūdaeōrum ut perīre potius quam cēdere māllent.
3 nēmō sciēbat utrum Haterius an Salvius rem administrāvisset.
4 uxor mihi persuāsit nē hoc susciperem.
5 extrā carcerem stābant decem mīlitēs quī captīvōs custōdīrent.

In each sentence, find the reason why a subjunctive is being used.

7 From Stage 33 onwards, you have met the subjunctive used with 'priusquam' (meaning 'before') and 'dum' (meaning 'until'):

Myropnous iānuam clausit priusquam mīlitēs intrārent.
Myropnous shut the door before the soldiers could enter.

exspectābam dum amīcus advenīret.
I was waiting until my friend should arrive.

    Or, in more natural English:
I was waiting for my friend to arrive.

Longer sentences

1 Study each sentence and answer the questions that follow it:

1 postquam Haterius fabrōs, quī labōrābant in āreā, dīmīsit, Salvius negōtium agere coepit.

Where were the craftsmen working? What did Haterius do to them? What did Salvius then do? Translate the sentence.

2 spectātōrēs, cum candēlābrum aureum ē templō Iūdaeōrum raptum cōnspexissent, iterum iterumque plausērunt.

What did the spectators catch sight of? Where had it been seized? What was the reaction of the spectators? Translate the sentence.

3 fūr, cum verba centuriōnis audīvisset, tantō metū poenārum affectus est ut pecūniam quam ē tabernā abstulerat, statim abicere cōnstitueret.

What did the thief hear? What were his feelings? What did he decide to do? Where had the money come from? Translate the sentence.

2 Further examples for study and translation:

1 ancillae, quod dominam vehementer clāmantem audīvērunt, cubiculum eius quam celerrimē petīvērunt.

2 equitēs adeō pugnāre cupiēbant ut, simulac dux signum dedit, ē portīs castrōrum ērumperent.

3 postquam cōnsul hanc sententiam dīxit, Domitiānus servō adstantī imperāvit ut epistulam ab Agricolā nūper missam recitāret.

PART TWO: Words and phrases

Notes

1 Nouns, adjectives and most verbs are listed as in the Unit IIIA Language Information section.

2 Prepositions used with the ablative, such as 'ex', are marked +*abl.*; those used with the accusative, such as 'per', are marked +*acc.*

3 Deponent verbs (met and explained in Stage 32) are listed in the following way:

the 1st person singular of the present tense. This always ends in '-or', e.g. cōnor ('I try');
the infinitive. This always ends in '-ī', e.g. cōnārī ('to try');
the 1st person singular of the perfect tense, e.g. cōnātus sum ('I tried');
the meaning.

So, if the following forms are given:

loquor, loquī, locūtus sum – speak

'loquor' means 'I speak', 'loquī' means 'to speak', 'locūtus sum' means 'I spoke'.

4 Study the following deponent verbs, listed in the way described in paragraph 3:

cōnspicor, cōnspicārī, cōnspicātus sum – catch sight of
ingredior, ingredī, ingressus sum – enter
lābor, lābī, lāpsus sum – fall

Give the meaning of:

cōnspicor, ingredī, lāpsus sum, ingredior, cōnspicātus sum, lābī.

5 Use the list on pages 156–181 to find the meaning of:

ēgredior, hortātus sum, pollicērī, sequor, minārī, adeptus sum.

6 All words which are given in the 'Words and phrases checklists' for Stages 1–34 are marked with an asterisk.

a

*ā, ab +*abl.* – from; by
* abeō, abīre, abiī – go away
abhinc – ago
abhorreō, abhorrēre, abhorruī –
shrink (from)
abigō, abigere, abēgī, abāctus –
drive away
absēns, *gen.* absentis – absent
absentia, absentiae, f. – absence
abstulī *see* auferō
* absum, abesse, āfuī – be out, be
absent, be away
* ac – and
* accidō, accidere, accidī – happen
* accipiō, accipere, accēpī, acceptus –
accept, take in, receive
* accūsō, accūsāre, accūsāvī, accūsātus
– accuse
* ācriter – keenly, eagerly, fiercely
āctus *see* agō
* ad +*acc.* – to, at
* addō, addere, addidī, additus – add
* adeō, adīre, adiī – approach, go up to
* adeō – so much, so greatly
adeptus *see* adipīscor
adest *see* adsum
adhibeō, adhibēre, adhibuī,
adhibitus – use, apply
precēs adhibēre – offer prayers to
* adhūc – up till now
* adipīscor, adipīscī, adeptus sum –
receive, obtain
* aditus, aditūs, m. – entrance
* adiuvō, adiuvāre, adiūvī – help
adligō, adligāre, adligāvī, adligātus –
tie
adloquor, adloquī, adlocūtus sum –
speak to, address
* administrō, administrāre,
administrāvī, administrātus –
look after, manage
admīrātiō, admīrātiōnis, f. –
admiration
admīror, admīrārī, admīrātus sum –
admire

admittō, admittere, admīsī, admissus
– admit, let in
adōrō, adōrāre, adōrāvī, adōrātus –
worship
* adstō, adstāre, adstitī – stand by
* adsum, adesse, adfuī – be here,
be present
* adveniō, advenīre, advēnī – arrive
* adventus, adventūs, m. – arrival
* adversus, adversa, adversum –
hostile, unfavourable
*   rēs adversae – misfortune
* aedificium, aedificiī, n. – building
* aedificō, aedificāre, aedificāvī,
aedificātus – build
* aeger, aegra, aegrum – sick, ill
aegrōtus, aegrōtī, m. – invalid
Aegyptus, Aegyptī, m. – Egypt
* aequus, aequa, aequum – fair, calm
*   aequō animō – calmly, in a calm
spirit
aeternus, aeterna, aeternum – eternal
Aethiopes, Aethiopum, m.pl. –
Ethiopians
* afficiō, afficere, affēcī, affectus – affect
affectus, affecta, affectum –
overcome, struck
afflīgō, afflīgere, afflīxī, afflīctus –
afflict, hurt
agellus, agellī, m. – small plot of land
agger, aggeris, m. – ramp, mound of
earth
* agitō, agitāre, agitāvī, agitātus –
chase, hunt
* agmen, agminis, n. – column (of
men), procession
* agnōscō, agnōscere, agnōvī, agnitus –
recognise
* agō, agere, ēgī, āctus – do, act
āctum est dē nōbīs – it's all over
with us
age! – come on!
*   fābulam agere – act a play
*   grātiās agere – thank, give thanks
*   negōtium agere – do business, work

vītam agere – lead a life
* agricola, agricolae, m. – farmer
  alacriter – eagerly
* aliquandō – sometimes
* aliquis, aliquid – someone, something
  aliquid mīrī – something
  extraordinary
* alius, alia, aliud – other, another,
  else
* aliī . . . aliī – some . . . others
* alter, altera, alterum – the other,
  another, a second, the second
  alter . . . alter – one . . . the other
* altus, alta, altum – high, deep
  ambitiō, ambitiōnis, f. – bribery,
  corruption
* ambō, ambae, ambō – both
* ambulō, ambulāre, ambulāvī – walk
  āmēns, *gen.* āmentis – out of one's
  mind, in a frenzy
* amīcus, amīcī, m. – friend
* āmittō, āmittere, āmīsī, āmissus –
  lose
* amō, amāre, amāvī, amātus – love,
  like
* amor, amōris, m. – love
  amphitheātrum, amphitheātrī, n. –
  amphitheatre
  amphora, amphorae, f. – wine-jar
* amplector, amplectī, amplexus sum –
  embrace
  amplissimus, amplissima,
  amplissimum – very great
  amputō, amputāre, amputāvī,
  amputātus – cut off
* ancilla, ancillae, f. – slave-girl, maid
  angelus, angelī, m. – angel
* angustus, angusta, angustum –
  narrow
  animadvertō, animadvertere,
  animadvertī, animadversus –
  notice, take notice of
* animus, animī, m. – spirit, soul, mind
* aequō animō – calmly, in a calm
  spirit
* in animō volvere – wonder, turn
  over in the mind

* annus, annī, m. – year
* ante + *acc.* – before, in front of
* anteā – before
* antīquus, antīqua, antīquum
  – old, ancient
* ānulus, ānulī, m. – ring
  anus, anūs, f. – old woman
  anxius, anxia, anxium – anxious
  aper, aprī, m. – boar
* aperiō, aperīre, aperuī, apertus –
  open
  apertē – openly
* appāreō, appārēre, appāruī – appear
* appellō, appellāre, appellāvī,
  appellātus – call, call out to
* appropinquō, appropinquāre,
  appropinquāvī –
  approach, come near to
  aptus, apta, aptum – suitable
* apud + *acc.* – among, at the house of
* aqua, aquae, f. – water
* āra, ārae, f. – altar
  arbiter, arbitrī, m. – expert, judge
* arcessō, arcessere, arcessīvī,
  arcessītus – summon, send for
  architectus, architectī, m. – builder,
  architect
  arcus, arcūs, m. – arch
* ardeō, ardēre, arsī – burn, be on fire
  ardor, ardōris, m. – spirit,
  enthusiasm
  ārea, āreae, f. – courtyard, building
  site
* argenteus, argentea, argenteum –
  made of silver
  armātus, armāta, armātum – armed
* arrogantia, arrogantiae, f. – cheek,
  arrogance
* ars, artis, f. – art, skill
  artifex, artificis, m. – artist, craftsman
  as, assis, m. – as (small coin)
* ascendō, ascendere, ascendī – climb,
  rise
* at – but
  Athēnae, Athēnārum, f.pl. – Athens
  Athēnīs – at Athens
* atque – and

* ātrium, ātriī, n. – hall
* attonitus, attonita, attonitum – astonished
* auctor, auctōris, m. – creator, originator, person responsible
  mē auctōre – at my suggestion
* auctōritās, auctōritātis, f. – authority
* audācia, audāciae, f. – boldness, audacity
  audācter – boldly
* audāx, *gen.* audācis – bold, daring
* audeō, audēre – dare
* audiō, audīre, audīvī, audītus – hear

* auferō, auferre, abstulī, ablātus – take away, steal
  augeō, augēre, auxī, auctus – increase
  augur, auguris, m. – augur
* aula, aulae, f. – palace
* aureus, aurea, aureum – golden, made of gold
  aurīga, aurīgae, m. – charioteer
* auris, auris, f. – ear
* autem – but
* auxilium, auxiliī, n. – help
* avārus, avārī, m. – miser
  avia, aviae, f. – grandmother
* avidē – eagerly
* avis, avis, f. – bird

b

balneum, balneī, n. – bath
* barbarus, barbarī, m. – barbarian
* bellum, bellī, n. – war
*   bellum gerere – wage war, campaign
* bene – well
*   optimē – very well
* beneficium, beneficiī, n. – act of kindness, favour
* benignus, benigna, benignum – kind
* bibō, bibere, bibī – drink

blandus, blanda, blandum – flattering, charming
* bonus, bona, bonum – good
*   melior, melius – better
    melius est – it would be better
*   optimus, optima, optimum – very good, excellent, best
    brevī – in a short time
* brevis, breve – short, brief
  Britannī, Britannōrum, m.pl. –. Britons
  Britannia, Britanniae, f. – Britain

c

C. = Gāius
cachinnō, cachinnāre, cachinnāvī – laugh, cackle
* caedō, caedere, cecīdī, caesus – kill
* caelum, caelī, n. – sky, heaven
  calceus, calceī, m. – shoe
* callidus, callida, callidum – clever, cunning, shrewd
  candēlābrum, candēlābrī, n. – lamp-stand, candelabrum
  candidātus, candidātī, m. – candidate
* canis, canis, m. – dog
* cantō, cantāre, cantāvī – sing, chant
  tībiīs cantāre – play on the pipes

* capiō, capere, cēpī, captus – take, catch, capture
  cōnsilium capere – make a plan, have an idea
  Capitōlium, Capitōliī, n. – Capitol
  captīva, captīvae, f. – (female) prisoner, captive
* captīvus, captīvī, m. – prisoner, captive
* caput, capitis, n. – head
* carcer, carceris, m. – prison
* carmen, carminis, n. – song
* cārus, cāra, cārum – dear
  castellum, castellī, n. – fort

* castīgō, castīgāre, castīgāvī,
  castīgātus – scold
* castra, castrōrum, n.pl. – camp
* cāsus, cāsūs, m. – misfortune
* catēna, catēnae, f. – chain
  caudex, caudicis, m. – blockhead,
  idiot
* cautē – cautiously
  caveō, cavēre, cāvī – beware
* cēdō, cēdere, cessī – give in, give way
* celebrō, celebrāre, celebrāvī,
  celebrātus – celebrate
* celeriter – quickly, fast
  quam celerrimē – as quickly as
  possible
  cellārius, cellāriī, m. – steward
* cēlō, cēlāre, cēlāvī, cēlātus – hide
* cēna, cēnae, f. – dinner
* cēnō, cēnāre, cēnāvī – dine, have
  dinner
* centum – a hundred
* centuriō, centuriōnis, m. – centurion
  cēpī *see* capiō
* cēra, cērae, f. – wax, wax tablet
* certāmen, certāminis, n. – struggle,
  fight
  certē – certainly
* certō, certāre, certāvī – compete
* cēterī, cēterae, cētera – the others,
  the rest
  Chrīstiānī, Chrīstiānōrum, m.pl. –
  Christians
* cibus, cibī, m. – food
* cinis, cineris, m. – ash
  circā +*acc.* – around
  circiter +*acc.* – about
  circulus, circulī, m. – hoop
* circum +*acc.* – around
* circumspectō, circumspectāre,
  circumspectāvī – look round
* circumveniō, circumvenīre,
  circumvēnī, circumventus –
  surround
  circus, circī, m. – circus, stadium
  citharoedus, citharoedī, m. – cithara
  player
* cīvis, cīvis, m.f. – citizen

clādēs, clādis, f. – disaster
* clāmō, clāmāre, clāmāvī – shout
* clāmor, clāmōris, m. – shout, uproar
* clārus, clāra, clārum – famous,
  distinguished
* claudō, claudere, clausī, clausus –
  shut, close, block, conclude,
  complete
* cliēns, clientis, m. – client
* coepī – I began
* cōgitō, cōgitāre, cōgitāvī – think,
  consider
* cognōscō, cognōscere, cognōvī,
  cognitus – get to know, find out
* cōgō, cōgere, coēgī, coāctus – force,
  compel
* cohors, cohortis, f. – cohort
* colligō, colligere, collēgī, collēctus –
  gather, collect, assemble
* collocō, collocāre, collocāvī,
  collocātus – place, put
* colloquium, colloquiī, n. – talk, chat
  columba, columbae, f. – dove
  columna, columnae, f. – pillar
* comes, comitis, m.f. – comrade,
  companion
  cōmiter – politely, courteously
* comitor, comitārī, comitātus sum –
  accompany
  comitāns, *gen.* comitantis –
  accompanying
* commemorō, commemorāre,
  commemorāvī, commemorātus
  – talk about, mention, recall
  commendō, commendāre,
  commendāvī, commendātus –
  recommend
  committō, committere, commīsī,
  commissus – commit, begin
* commodus, commoda, commodum –
  convenient
* commōtus, commōta, commōtum –
  moved, upset, affected, alarmed,
  excited, distressed, overcome
* comparō, comparāre, comparāvī,
  comparātus – obtain
  compitum, compitī, n. – crossroads

* compleō, complēre, complēvī,
  complētus – fill
compluvium, compluviī, n. –
  compluvium (opening in roof)
* compōnō, compōnere, composuī,
  compositus – put together,
  arrange, settle, mix, make up
compositus, composita,
  compositum – composed, steady
* comprehendō, comprehendere,
  comprehendī, comprehēnsus –
  arrest
cōnātus *see* cōnor
conciliō, conciliāre, conciliāvī,
  conciliātus – win, gain
conclāve, conclāvis, n. – room
concrepō, concrepāre, concrepuī –
  snap
* condūcō, condūcere, condūxī,
  conductus – hire
* cōnficiō, cōnficere, cōnfēcī, cōnfectus
  – finish
cōnfectus, cōnfecta, cōnfectum –
  worn out, exhausted, overcome
* cōnfīdō, cōnfīdere – trust, put trust
cōnfīsus, cōnfīsa, cōnfīsum –
  having trusted, having put trust
* coniciō, conicere, coniēcī, coniectus
  – hurl, throw
* coniūrātiō, coniūrātiōnis, f. –
  plot, conspiracy
* cōnor, cōnārī, cōnātus sum – try
* cōnscendō, cōnscendere, cōnscendī –
  climb on, embark on, go on
  board, mount
cōnscīscō, cōnscīscere, cōnscīvī –
  inflict
  mortem sibi cōnscīscere – commit
  suicide
* cōnsentiō, cōnsentīre, cōnsēnsī –
  agree
cōnsīdō, cōnsīdere, cōnsēdī – sit
  down
* cōnsilium, cōnsiliī, n. – plan, idea,
  advice
  cōnsilium capere – make a plan,
  have an idea

* cōnsistō, cōnsistere, cōnstitī – stand
  one's ground, stand firm, halt,
  stop
* cōnspiciō, cōnspicere, cōnspexī,
  cōnspectus – catch sight of
* cōnspicor, cōnspicārī, cōnspicātus
  sum – catch sight of
cōnspicuus, cōnspicua, cōnspicuum
  – conspicuous, easily seen
* cōnstituō, cōnstituere, cōnstituī,
  cōnstitūtus – decide
cōnsul, cōnsulis, m. – consul (senior
  magistrate)
* cōnsulātus, cōnsulātūs, m. –
  consulship (rank of consul)
* cōnsulō, cōnsulere, cōnsuluī,
  cōnsultus – consult
* cōnsūmō, cōnsūmere, cōnsūmpsī,
  cōnsūmptus – eat
* contendō, contendere, contendī –
  hurry
* contentus, contenta, contentum –
  satisfied
continuus, continua, continuum –
  continuous, on end
contiō, contiōnis, f. – speech
* contrā (1) +*acc.* – against
  (2) – on the other hand
contumēlia, contumēliae, f. – insult,
  abuse
convalēscō, convalēscere, convaluī –
  get better, recover
* conveniō, convenīre, convēnī –
  come together, gather, meet
* convertō, convertere, convertī,
  conversus – turn
convertor, convertī, conversus sum
  – turn
convīva, convīvae, m. – guest
convolvō, convolvere, convolvī,
  convolūtus – entangle
* coquō, coquere, coxī, coctus – cook
* coquus, coquī, m. – cook
* corōna, corōnae, f. – garland, wreath
* corpus, corporis, n. – body

corrumpō, corrumpere, corrūpī,
corruptus – corrupt
dōnīs corrumpere – bribe
* cotīdiē – every day
* crās – tomorrow
* crēdō, crēdere, crēdidī – trust,
believe, have faith in
* creō, creāre, creāvī, creātus – make,
create
crepidārius, crepidāriī, m. –
shoemaker
* crūdēlis, crūdēle – cruel
crux, crucis, f. – cross
* cubiculum, cubiculī, n. – bedroom
cucurrī *see* currō
cui, cuius *see* quī
culīna, culīnae, f. – kitchen
culpō, culpāre, culpāvī – blame
culter, cultrī, m. – knife

* cum (1) – when
* cum (2) +*abl.* – with
cumulō, cumulāre, cumulāvī,
cumulātus – heap
cumulus, cumulī, m. – pile, heap
* cupiō, cupere, cupīvī – want
* cūr? – why?
* cūra, cūrae, f. – care
cūrae esse – be a matter of concern
cūria, cūriae, f. – senate-house
* cūrō, cūrāre, cūrāvī – look after,
supervise
* currō, currere, cucurrī – run
currus, currūs, m. – chariot
* cursus, cursūs, m. – course, flight
* custōdiō, custōdīre, custōdīvī,
custōdītus – guard
* custōs, custōdis, m. – guard

d

* damnō, damnāre, damnāvī,
damnātus – condemn
dare *see* dō
* dē +*abl.* – from, down from; about
* dea, deae, f. – goddess
* dēbeō, dēbēre, dēbuī, dēbitus – owe;
ought, should, must
* decem – ten
* decet, decēre, decuit – be proper
nōs decet – we ought
* dēcidō, dēcidere, dēcidī – fall down
* decimus, decima, decimum – tenth
* dēcipiō, dēcipere, dēcēpī, dēceptus –
deceive, trick
dēclārō, dēclārāre, dēclārāvī,
dēclārātus – declare, proclaim
* decōrus, decōra, decōrum – right,
proper
dedī *see* dō
dēdicō, dēdicāre, dēdicāvī, dēdicātus
– dedicate
dēdūcō, dēdūcere, dēdūxī, dēductus
– escort

* dēfendō, dēfendere, dēfendī, dēfēnsus
– defend
* dēfessus, dēfessa, dēfessum –
exhausted, tired out
dēfigō, dēfigere, dēfīxī, dēfīxus – fix
* dēiciō, dēicere, dēiēcī, dēiectus –
throw down, throw
dēiectus, dēiecta, dēiectum –
disappointed, downcast
* deinde – then
* dēlectō, dēlectāre, dēlectāvī,
dēlectātus – delight, please
* dēleō, dēlēre, dēlēvī, dēlētus – destroy
dēliciae, dēliciārum, f.pl. – darling
dēligō, dēligāre, dēligāvī, dēligātus –
bind, tie, tie up, moor
* dēmittō, dēmittere, dēmīsī, dēmissus
– let down, lower
* dēmōnstrō, dēmōnstrāre,
dēmōnstrāvī, dēmōnstrātus –
point out, show
dēmoveō, dēmovēre, dēmōvī, dēmōtus
– dismiss, move out of way

dēmum – at last
tum dēmum – then at last, only
then
dēnārius, dēnāriī, m. – denarius (coin
worth four sesterces)
*dēnique – at last, finally
dēns, dentis, m. – tooth, tusk
* dēnsus, dēnsa, dēnsum – thick
dēpellō, dēpellere, dēpulī, dēpulsus –
drive off, push down
* dēpōnō, dēpōnere, dēposuī, dēpositus
– put down, take off
dēprōmō, dēprōmere, dēprōmpsī,
dēprōmptus – bring out
* dērīdeō, dērīdēre, dērīsī, dērīsus –
mock, jeer at
* dēscendō, dēscendere, dēscendī –
go down, come down
* dēserō, dēserere, dēseruī, dēsertus –
desert
* dēsiliō, dēsilīre, dēsiluī – jump
down
* dēsinō, dēsinere – end, cease
dēsistō, dēsistere, dēstitī – stop
* dēspērō, dēspērāre, dēspērāvī –
despair, give up
dēspiciō, dēspicere, dēspexī – look
down
dēstringō, dēstringere, dēstrīnxī,
dēstrictus – draw out, draw
(a sword), unsheathe
dētestor, dētestārī, dētestātus sum –
curse
dētrahō, dētrahere, dētrāxī, dētractus
– pull down
* deus, deī, m. – god
* dī immortālēs! – heavens above!
dēvorō, dēvorāre, dēvorāvī,
dēvorātus – devour, eat up
dī see deus
diabolus, diabolī, m. – devil
* dīcō, dīcere, dīxī, dictus – say
* dictō, dictāre, dictāvī, dictātus –
dictate
* diēs, diēī, m. – day
diēs fēstus, diēī fēstī, m. – festival,
holiday

* diēs nātālis, diēī nātālis, m. –
birthday
* difficilis, difficile – difficult
difficultās, difficultātis, f. – difficulty
digitus, digitī, m. – finger
* dignitās, dignitātis, f. – dignity,
importance, honour, prestige
* dīligenter – carefully
* dīligentia, dīligentiae, f. – industry,
hard work
* dīligō, dīligere, dīlēxī – be fond of
* dīmittō, dīmittere, dīmīsī, dīmissus –
send away, dismiss
dīripiō, dīripere, dīripuī, dīreptus –
pull apart, ransack
* dīrus, dīra, dīrum – dreadful
dīs see deus
* discēdō, discēdere, discessī – depart,
leave
discipulus, discipulī, m. – disciple,
follower
discō, discere, didicī – learn
discordia, discordiae, f. – strife
discrīmen, discrīminis, n. – crisis
* dissentiō, dissentīre, dissēnsī –
disagree, argue
dissimulō, dissimulāre, dissimulāvī,
dissimulātus – conceal, hide
distribuō, distribuere, distribuī,
distribūtus – distribute
* diū – for a long time
* dīves, gen. dīvitis – rich
dītissimus, dītissima, dītissimum –
very rich
* dīvitiae, dīvitiārum, f.pl. – riches
dīvus, dīvī, m. – god
dīxī see dīcō
* dō, dare, dedī, datus – give
* poenās dare – pay the penalty, be
punished
* doceō, docēre, docuī, doctus – teach
* doctus, docta, doctum – learned,
educated, skilful, clever
* doleō, dolēre, doluī – hurt, be in pain
* dolor, dolōris, m. – pain, grief
* domina, dominae, f. – mistress
* dominus, dominī, m. – master

*domus, domūs, f. – home
  domī – at home
  domum redīre – return home
*dōnum, dōnī, n. – present, gift
  dōnīs corrumpere – bribe
*dormiō, dormīre, dormīvī – sleep
*dubium, dubiī, n. – doubt
*ducentī, ducentae, ducenta – two
  hundred

*dūcō, dūcere, dūxī, ductus – lead
  sorte ductus – chosen by lot
*dulcis, dulce – sweet
*dum – while, until
*duo, duae, duo – two
  duodecim – twelve
*dūrus, dūra, dūrum – harsh, hard
*dux, ducis, m. – leader
  dūxī *see* dūcō

e

*ē, ex +*abl.* – from, out of
ea, eā, eam *see* is
eandem – the same
eās *see* is
ēbrius, ēbria, ēbrium – drunk
*ecce! – see! look!
edō, edere, ēdī, ēsus – eat
ēdō, ēdere, ēdidī, ēditus – put on,
  present
efferō, efferre, extulī, ēlātus – bring
  out, carry out
ēlātus, ēlāta, ēlātum – thrilled,
  excited
*efficiō, efficere, effēcī, effectus – carry
  out, accomplish
*effigiēs, effigiēī, f. – image, statue
effringō, effringere, effrēgī, effrāctus –
  break down
*effugiō, effugere, effūgī – escape
*effundō, effundere, effūdī, effūsus –
  pour out
  effūsīs lacrimīs – bursting into tears
ēgī *see* agō
*ego, meī – I, me
  mēcum – with me
*ēgredior, ēgredī, ēgressus sum – go
  out
*ēheu! – alas!
eī *see* is
*ēiciō, ēicere, ēiēcī, ēiectus – throw out
eīs, eius *see* is
eiusmodī – of that kind
ēlābor, ēlābī, ēlāpsus sum – escape
ēlātus *see* efferō

ēlegāns, *gen.* ēlegantis – tasteful,
  elegant
ēlegantia, ēlegantiae, f. – good taste,
  elegance
ēliciō, ēlicere, ēlicuī, ēlicitus – lure,
  entice
*ēligō, ēligere, ēlēgī, ēlēctus – choose
ēlūdō, ēlūdere, ēlūdī, ēlūsus – slip
  past, trick, outwit
*ēmittō, ēmittere, ēmīsī, ēmissus –
  throw, send out
*emō, emere, ēmī, ēmptus – buy
ēmoveō, ēmovēre, ēmōvī, ēmōtus –
  move, clear away, remove
ēn! – look!
  ēn Rōmānī! – so these are the
  Romans!
*enim – for
*eō, īre, iī – go
  obviam īre – meet, go to meet
  eō *see* is
eōdem – the same
eōrum, eōs *see* is
*epistula, epistulae, f. – letter
epulae, epulārum, f.pl. – dishes
*eques, equitis, m. – horseman; man of
  equestrian rank
*equitō, equitāre, equitāvī – ride
*equus, equī, m. – horse
eram *see* sum
ergō – therefore
*errō, errāre, errāvī – make a mistake
ērubēscō, ērubēscere, ērubuī – blush

ērumpō, ērumpere, ērūpī – break
away, break out
est, estō *see* sum
* et – and
*   et ... et – both ... and
* etiam – even, also
nōn modo ... sed etiam – not only
...but also
* euge! – hurray!
eum *see* is
evangelium, evangeliī, n. – good
news, gospel
ēvertō, ēvertere, ēvertī, ēversus –
overturn
ēvolō, ēvolāre, ēvolāvī – fly out
* ex, ē + *abl.* – from, out of
* exanimātus, exanimāta,
exanimātum – unconscious
* excipiō, excipere, excēpī, exceptus –
receive
* excitō, excitāre, excitāvī, excitātus –
arouse, wake up, awaken
* exclāmō, exclāmāre, exclāmāvī –
exclaim, shout
excūdō, excūdere, excūdī, excūsus –
forge, hammer out
exemplum, exemplī, n. – example
* exeō, exīre, exiī – go out
* exerceō, exercēre, exercuī, exercitus –
exercise

exīstimō, exīstimāre, exīstimāvī,
exīstimātus – think, consider
* exitium, exitiī, n. – ruin, destruction
* explicō, explicāre, explicāvī,
explicātus – explain
expōnō, expōnere, exposuī, expositus
– unload
expugnō, expugnāre, expugnāvī,
expugnātus – storm, take by
storm
exquīsītus, exquīsīta, exquīsītum –
special
* exspectō, exspectāre, exspectāvī,
exspectātus – wait for
* exstinguō, exstinguere, exstīnxī,
exstīnctus – extinguish, put out,
destroy
* exstruō, exstruere, exstrūxī,
exstrūctus – build
exsultō, exsultāre, exsultāvī – exult,
be triumphant
exta, extōrum, n.pl. – entrails
* extrā – outside
* extrahō, extrahere, extrāxī, extractus
– drag out, pull out, take out
extrēmus, extrēma, extrēmum –
furthest
extrēma pars – edge
extulī *see* efferō

f

* faber, fabrī, m. – craftsman,
carpenter, workman
* fābula, fābulae, f. – play, story
*   fābulam agere – act a play
facēs *see* fax
* facile – easily
* facilis, facile – easy
* facinus, facinoris, n. – crime
* faciō, facere, fēcī, factus – make, do
floccī nōn faciō – I don't care a
hang for
factum, factī, n. – deed, achievement
factus *see* fīō

* falsus, falsa, falsum – false, untrue,
dishonest
famēs, famis, f. – hunger
* familiāris, familiāris, m. – close
friend, relation, relative
faucēs, faucium, f.pl. – passage,
entrance-way
* faveō, favēre, fāvī – favour, support
* favor, favōris, m. – favour
* fax, facis, f. – torch
fēcī *see* faciō
fēlēs, fēlis, f. – cat
fēlīx, *gen.* fēlīcis – lucky, happy

* fēmina, fēminae, f. – woman
* ferō, ferre, tulī, lātus – bring, carry
* ferōciter – fiercely
* ferōx, *gen.* ferōcis – fierce, ferocious
  ferrārius, ferrāriī, m. – blacksmith
* ferrum, ferrī, n. – iron, sword
* fessus, fessa, fessum – tired
* festīnō, festīnāre, festīnāvī – hurry
* fēstus, fēsta, fēstum – festival, holiday
* fidēlis, fidēle – faithful, loyal
* fidēs, fideī, f. – loyalty,
  trustworthiness
  fidem servāre – keep a promise,
  keep faith
  fīgō, fīgere, fīxī, fīxus – fix, fasten
  figūra, figūrae, f. – figure, shape
* fīlia, fīliae, f. – daughter
* fīlius, fīliī, m. – son
  fīnis, fīnis, m. – end
  fīō – I become
  factus sum – I became
  fīxus *see* fīgō
  flāgitō, flāgitāre, flāgitāvī – nag at,
  put pressure on
  flagrō, flagrāre, flagrāvī – blaze
* flamma, flammae, f. - flame
  floccī nōn faciō – I don't care a
  hang for
* flōs, flōris, m. – flower
* flūmen, flūminis, n. – river
* fluō, fluere, flūxī – flow
* fōns, fontis, m. – fountain, spring

  fōrma, fōrmae, f. – beauty,
  appearance
* fortasse – perhaps
* forte – by chance
* fortis, forte – brave
* fortiter – bravely
  fortitūdō, fortitūdinis, f. – courage
* fortūna, fortūnae, f. – fortune, luck
  fortūnātus, fortūnāta, fortūnātum –
  lucky
* forum, forī, n. – forum, market-place
* fossa, fossae, f. – ditch
  fragor, fragōris, m. – crash
* frangō, frangere, frēgī, frāctus –
  break
* frāter, frātris, m. – brother
* fraus, fraudis, f. – trick
  frōns, frontis, f. – front
* frūmentum, frūmentī, n. – grain
* frūstrā – in vain
* fuga, fugae, f. – escape
* fugiō, fugere, fūgī – run away,
  flee (from)
  fuī *see* sum
* fulgeō, fulgēre, fulsī – shine, glitter
* fundō, fundere, fūdī, fūsus – pour
* fundus, fundī, m. – farm
  fūnis, fūnis, m. – rope
* fūr, fūris, m. – thief
* furēns, *gen.* furentis – furious, in a
  rage
  fūrtum, fūrtī, n. – theft, robbery
  fūstis, fūstis, m. – club, stick

g

* gaudeō, gaudēre – be pleased, rejoice
* gaudium, gaudiī, n. – joy
  gāza, gāzae, f. – treasure
* geminī, geminōrum, m.pl. – twins
* gemitus, gemitūs, m. – groan
* gemma, gemmae, f. – jewel, gem
* gēns, gentis, f. – family, tribe
* gerō, gerere, gessī, gestus – wear
*   bellum gerere – wage war,
  campaign
  gladiātor, gladiātōris, m. – gladiator

* gladius, gladiī, m. – sword
  glōria, glōriae, f. – glory
  glōriāns, *gen.* glōriantis – boasting,
  boastfully
  Graecia, Graeciae, f. – Greece
  Graecus, Graeca, Graecum – Greek
  grātiae, grātiārum, f.pl. – thanks
*   grātiās agere – thank, give thanks
  grātīs – free
  grātulātiō, grātulātiōnis, f. –
  congratulation

grātulor, grātulārī, grātulātus sum –
  congratulate
grātulāns, *gen.* grātulantis –
  congratulating

h

* habeō, habēre, habuī, habitus – have
* habitō, habitāre, habitāvī – live
* haereō, haerēre, haesī – stick, cling
* haesitō, haesitāre, haesitāvī – hesitate
* haruspex, haruspicis, m. – soothsayer
* hasta, hastae, f. – spear
* haud – not
* haudquāquam – not at all
* hauriō, haurīre, hausī, haustus –
    drain, drink up
* hercle! – by Hercules!
* hērēs, hērēdis, m.f. – heir
* heri – yesterday
* hic, haec, hoc – this
* hīc – here
* hiems, hiemis, f. – winter
    hinc – from here
* hodiē – today
* homō, hominis, m. – man
    homunculus, homunculī, m. – little
      man

* gravis, grave – heavy, serious
* graviter – heavily, soundly, seriously
* gustō, gustāre, gustāvī – taste

* honor, honōris, m. – honour, official
    position
* honōrō, honōrāre, honōrāvī,
    honōrātus – honour
* hōra, hōrae, f. – hour
* horreum, horreī, n. – barn, granary
* hortor, hortārī, hortātus sum –
    encourage, urge
* hortus, hortī, m. – garden
* hospes, hospitis, m. – guest, host
* hostis, hostis, m.f. – enemy
* hūc – here, to this place
    hūc illūc – here and there, up and
      down
    huic, huius *see* hic
    humilis, humile – low-born, of low
      class
    humus, humī, f. – ground
*   humī – on the ground
      humum – to the ground

i

* iaceō, iacēre, iacuī – lie
* iaciō, iacere, iēcī, iactus – throw
* iactō, iactāre, iactāvī, iactātus –
    throw
* iam – now
    iamdūdum – for a long time
* iānua, iānuae, f. – door
    ībam *see* eō
* ibi – there
    id *see* is
* īdem, eadem, idem – the same
* identidem – repeatedly
    Ierosolyma, Ierosolymae, f. –
      Jerusalem

* igitur – therefore, and so
* ignārus, ignāra, ignārum – not
    knowing, unaware
* ignāvus, ignāva, ignāvum – lazy,
    cowardly
    ignis, ignis, m. – fire
    ignōrō, ignōrāre, ignōrāvī – not
      know of
* ignōscō, ignōscere, ignōvī – forgive
    iī *see* eō
* ille, illa, illud – that, he, she
* illūc – there, to that place
    hūc illūc – here and there, up and
      down

illūcēscō, illūcēscere, illūxī – dawn,
grow bright

imitor, imitārī, imitātus sum –
imitate, mime

*immemor, *gen.* immemoris – forgetful

*immineō, imminēre, imminuī – hang
over

immo – or rather

*immortālis, immortāle – immortal

* dī immortālēs! – heavens above!

immortālitās, immortālitātis, f. –
immortality

*immōtus, immōta, immōtum – still,
motionless

impatiēns, *gen.* impatientis –
impatient

*impediō, impedīre, impedīvī,
impedītus – delay, hinder

*imperātor, imperātōris, m. – emperor

*imperium, imperiī, n. – empire

*imperō, imperāre, imperāvī – order,
command

*impetus, impetūs, m. – attack

*impōnō, impōnere, imposuī,
impositus – impose, put into, put
onto

importō, importāre, importāvī,
importātus – import

impudēns, *gen.* impudentis –
shameless

*in (1) + *acc.* – into, onto
(2) +*abl.* – in, on

*incēdō, incēdere, incessī – march,
stride

*incendō, incendere, incendī, incēnsus
– burn, set fire to

incertus, incerta, incertum –
uncertain

*incidō, incidere, incidī – fall

*incipiō, incipere, incēpī, inceptus –
begin

*incitō, incitāre, incitāvī, incitātus –
urge on, encourage

inde – then

*indicium, indiciī, n. – sign, evidence

indignus, indigna, indignum –
unworthy, undeserved

indulgeō, indulgēre, indulsī – give way

*induō, induere, induī, indūtus – put
on

*īnfāns, īnfantis, m. – child, baby

*īnfēlīx, *gen.* īnfēlīcis – unlucky

*īnferō, īnferre, intulī, inlātus – bring
in, bring on, bring against

iniūriam īnferre – do an injustice to,
bring injury to

*īnfestus, īnfesta, īnfestum – hostile,
dangerous

īnfīgō, īnfīgere, īnfīxī, īnfīxus – fasten
onto

īnflīgō, īnflīgere, īnflīxī, īnflīctus –
inflict

īnflō, īnflāre, īnflāvī – blow

īnfundō, īnfundere, īnfūdī, īnfūsus –
pour into

*ingenium, ingeniī, n. – character

*ingēns, *gen.* ingentis – huge

*ingredior, ingredī, ingressus sum –
enter

*iniciō, inicere, iniēcī, iniectus – throw in

*inimīcus, inimīcī, m. – enemy

*iniūria, iniūriae, f. – injustice, injury

iniūriam īnferre – do an injustice
to, bring injury to

inlātus *see* īnferō

innītor, innītī, innīxus sum – lean, rest

inopia, inopiae, f. – poverty

inopīnātus, inopīnāta, inopīnātum –
unexpected

*inquit – says, said

īnsāniō, īnsānīre, īnsānīvī – be mad,
be insane

*īnsānus, īnsāna, īnsānum – mad,
crazy, insane

īnscrībō, īnscrībere, īnscrīpsī,
īnscrīptus – write, inscribe

*īnsidiae, īnsidiārum, f.pl. – trap,
ambush

īnsolēns, *gen.* īnsolentis – rude,
insolent

*īnspiciō, īnspicere, īnspexī, īnspectus
– look at, inspect, examine,
search

*īnstruō, īnstruere, īnstrūxī, īnstrūctus
 – draw up, set up
*īnsula, īnsulae, f. – island; block of
 flats
*intellegō, intellegere, intellēxī,
 intellēctus – understand
*intentē – intently
*inter + acc. – among
 inter sē – among themselves, with
 each other
*intereā – meanwhile
*interficiō, interficere, interfēcī,
 interfectus – kill
 interrogō, interrogāre, interrogāvī,
 interrogātus – question
 interrumpō, interrumpere, interrūpī,
 interruptus – interrupt
*intrō, intrāre, intrāvī – enter
 intulī see īnferō
*inveniō, invenīre, invēnī, inventus –
 find
 invicem – in turn
*invītō, invītāre, invītāvī, invītātus –
 invite
*invītus, invīta, invītum – unwilling,
 reluctant
*iocus, iocī, m. – joke
 Iovis see Iuppiter
*ipse, ipsa, ipsum – himself, herself,
 itself

*īra, īrae, f. – anger
*īrātus, īrāta, īrātum – angry
 īre see eō
*irrumpō, irrumpere, irrūpī – burst in,
 burst into
*is, ea, id – he, she, it
*iste, ista, istud – that
*ita – in this way
*ita vērō – yes
 Ītalia, Ītaliae, f. – Italy
*itaque – and so
*iter, itineris, n. – journey, progress
*iterum – again
*iubeō, iubēre, iussī, iussus – order
 Iūdaeī, Iūdaeōrum, m.pl. – Jews
 Iūdaeus, Iūdaea, Iūdaeum – Jewish
*iūdex, iūdicis, m. – judge
 iūdicō, iūdicāre, iūdicāvī, iūdicātus –
 judge
 iugulum, iugulī, n. – throat
 Iuppiter, Iovis, m. – Jupiter (god of
 the sky, greatest of Roman gods)
 iussī see iubeō
*iussum, iussī, n. – order, instruction
 iussū Silvae – at Silva's order
 iuvat, iuvāre – please
 mē iuvat – it pleases me
*iuveris, iuvenis, m. – young man
 iuxtā + acc. – next to

1

L. = Lūcius
lābor, lābī, lāpsus sum – fall
*labor, labōris, m. – work
*labōrō, labōrāre, labōrāvī – work
 labrum, labrī, n. – lip
*lacrima, lacrimae, f. – tear
 lacrimīs effūsīs – bursting into
 tears
*lacrimō, lacrimāre, lacrimāvī – weep,
 cry
 lacus, lacūs, m. – lake
*laedō, laedere, laesī, laesus – harm

 laetē – happily
*laetus, laeta, laetum – happy
 lānx, lancis, f. – dish
 lāpsus see lābī
 latebrae, latebrārum, f.pl. – hiding-
 place
*lateō, latēre, latuī – lie hidden
 later, lateris, m. – brick
*latrō, latrōnis, m. – robber
*lātus, lāta, lātum – wide
*laudō, laudāre, laudāvī, laudātus –
 praise

laurus, laurī, f. – laurel tree
* lavō, lavāre, lāvī, lautus – wash
* lectīca, lectīcae, f. – sedan-chair
lectīcārius, lectīcāriī, m. –
    chair-carrier, sedan-chair
    carrier
* lectus, lectī, m. – couch, bed
* lēgātus, lēgātī, m. – commander
* legiō, legiōnis, f. – legion
* legō, legere, lēgī, lēctus – read
lēniō, lēnīre, lēnīvī, lēnītus – soothe,
    calm down
* lēniter – gently
* lentē – slowly
* leō, leōnis, m. – lion
* libenter – gladly
* liber, librī, m. – book
* līberālis, līberāle – generous
* līberī, līberōrum, m.pl. – children
* līberō, līberāre, līberāvī, līberātus –
    free, set free
* lībertās, lībertātis, f. – freedom
* lībertus, lībertī, m. – freedman,
    ex-slave

Augustī lībertus – freedman of
    Augustus, freedman of the
    emperor
librum *see* liber
līmen, līminis, n. – threshold,
    doorway
* lingua, linguae, f. – tongue
littera, litterae, f. – letter
* lītus, lītoris, n. – sea-shore, shore
* locus, locī, m. – place
locūtus *see* loquor
longurius, longuriī, m. – pole
* longus, longa, longum – long
* loquor, loquī, locūtus sum – speak
lūbricus, lūbrica, lūbricum – slippery
lūcem *see* lūx
lūceō, lūcēre, lūxī – shine
lucerna, lucernae, f. – lamp
lūdō, lūdere, lūsī – play
* lūdus, lūdī, m. – game
lūgeō, lūgēre, lūxī – lament, mourn
* lūna, lūnae, f. – moon
lutum, lutī, n. – mud
* lūx, lūcis, f. – light, daylight

m

M. = Marcus
* magister, magistrī, m. – master,
    foreman
magistrātus, magistrātūs, m. –
    magistrate (elected official of
    Roman government)
magnificē – splendidly, magnificently
magnificus, magnifica, magnificum –
    splendid, magnificent
* magnopere – greatly
*   maximē – very greatly, very much,
    most of all
* magnus, magna, magnum – big,
    large, great
maior, *gen.* maiōris – bigger,
    larger, greater
*   maximus, maxima, maximum –
    very big, very large, very great,
    greatest

Pontifex Maximus – Chief Priest
malignus, maligna, malignum –
    spiteful
* mālō, mālle, māluī – prefer
* malus, mala, malum – evil, bad
*   pessimus, pessima, pessimum –
    very bad, worst
* mandātum, mandātī, n. – instruction,
    order
* mandō, mandāre, mandāvī,
    mandātus – order, entrust,
    hand over
* māne – in the morning
* maneō, manēre, mānsī – remain, stay
manifestus, manifesta, manifestum
    – clear
* manus, manūs, f. – hand; band
* mare, maris, n. – sea
margō, marginis, m. – edge

* marītus, marītī, m. – husband
marmor, marmoris, n. – marble
Mārs, Mārtis, m. – Mars (god of war)
massa, massae, f. – block
* māter, mātris, f. – mother
mātrōna, mātrōnae, f. – lady
maximē *see* magnopere
maximus *see* magnus
mē *see* ego
medicāmentum, medicāmentī, n. –
ointment, medicine, drug
* medicus, medicī, m. – doctor
* medius, media, medium – middle
melior *see* bonus
memor, *gen.* memoris –
remembering, mindful of
* mendāx, mendācis, m. – liar
mendāx, *gen.* mendācis – lying,
deceitful
mendīcus, mendīcī, m. – beggar
mēns, mentis, f. – mind
* mēnsa, mēnsae, f. – table
* mercātor, mercātōris, m. – merchant
* metus, metūs, m. – fear
* meus, mea, meum – my, mine
meī, meōrum, m.pl. – my family
mī Haterī – my dear Haterius
mihi *see* ego
* mīles, mīlitis, m. – soldier
* mīlle – a thousand
* mīlia – thousands
* minimē – no, least, very little
minimus *see* parvus
minister, ministrī, m. – servant, agent
minor *see* parvus
minor, minārī, minātus sum –
threaten
* mīrābilis, mīrābile – marvellous,
strange, wonderful
mīrus, mīra, mīrum – extraordinary
* miser, misera, miserum – miserable,
wretched, sad
* mittō, mittere, mīsī, missus – send
moderātus, moderāta, moderātum –
restrained, moderate

* modo – just, now, only
modo . . . modo – now . . . now
nōn modo . . . sed etiam – not only
. . . but also
* modus, modī, m. – manner, way, kind
* quō modō? – how? in what way?
* molestus, molesta, molestum –
troublesome
molliō, mollīre, mollīvī, mollītus
– soothe
mollis, molle – soft, gentle
* moneō, monēre, monuī, monitus –
warn, advise
* mōns, montis, m. – mountain
mora, morae, f. – delay
* morbus, morbī, m. – illness
* morior, morī, mortuus sum – die
moriēns, *gen.* morientis – dying
* mortuus, mortua, mortuum – dead
moror, morārī, morātus sum – delay
* mors, mortis, f. – death
mortem sibi cōnscīscere – commit
suicide
mortuus *see* morior
* mōs, mōris, m. – custom
mōtus, mōtūs, m. – movement
* moveō, movēre, mōvī, mōtus – move
* mox – soon
* multitūdō, multitūdinis, f. – crowd
* multō – much
multum – much
* multus, multa, multum – much
* multī – many
* plūrimī, plūrimae, plūrima – very
many
* plūrimus, plūrima, plūrimum –
most
plūris est – is worth more
* plūs, *gen.* plūris – more
plūs vīnī – more wine
mūnītiō, mūnītiōnis, f. – defence,
fortification
* mūrus, mūrī, m. – wall
mūs, mūris, m.f. – mouse
mussitō, mussitāre, mussitāvī –
murmur

n

nactus, nacta, nactum – having
   seized
* nam – for
* nārrō, nārrāre, nārrāvī, nārrātus –
   tell, relate
* nāscor, nāscī, nātus sum – be born
   nātū maximus – eldest
   trīgintā annōs nātus – thirty years
   old
* (diēs) nātālis, (diēī) nātālis, m. –
   birthday
   nātus see nāscor
* nauta, nautae, m. – sailor
* nāvigō, nāvigāre, nāvigāvī – sail
* nāvis, nāvis, f. – ship
   nē – that . . . not, so that . . . not
*   nē . . . quidem – not even
   nec – and not, nor
* necesse – necessary
* necō, necāre, necāvī, necātus – kill
* neglegēns, gen. neglegentis – careless
* neglegō, neglegere, neglēxī, neglēctus
   – neglect
* negōtium, negōtiī, n. – business
*   negōtium agere – do business, work
* nēmō – no one, nobody
   neque – and not, nor
*   neque . . . neque – neither . . . nor
* nescio, nescīre, nescīvī – not know
* nihil – nothing
* nihilōminus – nevertheless
* nimis – too
* nimium – too much
* nisi – except, unless
* nōbilis, nōbile – noble, of noble birth
   nōbīs see nōs

* noceō, nocēre, nocuī – hurt
   noctis see nox
* nōlō, nōlle, nōluī – not want
   nōlī, nōlīte – do not, don't
* nōmen, nōminis, n. – name
* nōn – not
* nōnāgintā – ninety
   nōndum – not yet
* nōnne? – surely?
* nōnnūllī, nōnnūllae, nōnnūlla –
   some, several
* nōnus, nōna, nōnum – ninth
* nōs – we, us
* noster, nostra, nostrum – our
   notō, notāre, notāvī, notātus – note,
   observe
* nōtus, nōta, nōtum – known,
   well-known, famous
* novem – nine
* nōvī – I know
* novus, nova, novum – new
* nox, noctis, f. – night
* nūbēs, nūbis, f. – cloud
* nūllus, nūlla, nūllum – not any, no
* num? – (1) surely . . . not?
* num – (2) whether
* numerō, numerāre, numerāvī,
   numerātus – count
* numerus, numerī, m. – number
* numquam – never
* nunc – now
* nūntiō, nūntiāre, nūntiāvī, nūntiātus
   – announce
* nūntius, nūntiī, m. – messenger,
   message, news
* nūper – recently
* nusquam – nowhere

o

obeō, obīre, obiī – meet, go to meet
obēsus, obēsa, obēsum – fat
obiciō, obicere, obiēcī, obiectus –
   present

oblītus, oblīta, oblītum – having
   forgotten
* obscūrus, obscūra, obscūrum – dark,
   gloomy

* obstō, obstāre, obstitī – obstruct,
  block the way
* obstupefaciō, obstupefacere,
  obstupefēcī, obstupefactus –
  amaze, stun
  obtulī *see* offerō
* obviam eō, obviam īre, obviam iī –
  meet, go to meet
  occāsiō, occāsiōnis, f. – opportunity
* occīdō, occīdere, occīdī, occīsus – kill
  occidō, occidere, occidī – set
* occupātus, occupāta, occupātum –
  busy
* occupō, occupāre, occupāvī,
  occupātus – seize, take over
* occurrō, occurrere, occurrī – meet
* octāvus, octāva, octāvum – eighth
* octō – eight
* octōgintā – eighty
* oculus, oculī, m. – eye
* ōdī – I hate
* odiō sum, odiō esse – be hateful
* offerō, offerre, obtulī, oblātus – offer
  oleum, oleī, n. – oil
* ōlim – once, some time ago
  ōmen, ōminis, n. – omen (sign from
  the gods)
* omnīnō – completely
* omnis, omne – all
  omnia – all, everything
* opēs, opum, f.pl. – money, wealth
* oportet, oportēre, oportuit – be right
  mē oportet – I must

* oppidum, oppidī, n. – town
* opprimō, opprimere, oppressī,
  oppressus – crush
* oppugnō, oppugnāre, oppugnāvī,
  oppugnātus – attack
  optimē *see* bene
  optimus *see* bonus
* opus, operis, n. – work, construction
  ōrātiō, ōrātiōnis, f. – speech
  orbis, orbis, m. – globe
  orbis terrārum – world
* ōrdō, ōrdinis, m. – row, line
  orior, orīrī, ortus sum – rise
  ōrnāmentum, ōrnāmentī, n. –
  ornament, decoration
  ōrnāmenta praetōria – honorary
  praetorship, honorary rank of
  praetor
  ōrnātus, ōrnāta, ōrnātum –
  decorated, elaborately furnished
* ōrnō, ōrnāre, ōrnāvī, ōrnātus –
  decorate
* ōrō, ōrāre, ōrāvī – beg
  ortus *see* orior
* ōs, ōris, n. – face
* ōsculum, ōsculī, n. – kiss
* ostendō, ostendere, ostendī, ostentus
  – show
  ostentō, ostentāre, ostentāvī,
  ostentātus – show off, display
* ōtiōsus, ōtiōsa, ōtiōsum – idle, on
  holiday, on vacation

p

* paene – nearly, almost
* pallēscō, pallēscere, palluī – grow
  pale
* pallidus, pallida, pallidum – pale
  pantomīmus, pantomīmī, m. –
  pantomimus, dancer
* parātus, parāta, parātum – ready,
  prepared
* parcō, parcere, pepercī – spare
* parēns, parentis, m.f. – parent

* pāreō, pārēre, pāruī – obey
* parō, parāre, parāvī, parātus –
  prepare
* pars, partis, f. – part
  extrēma pars – edge
  in prīmā parte – in the forefront
* parvus, parva, parvum – small
  minor, *gen.* minōris – less, smaller
*   minimus, minima, minimum –
  very little, least

passus *see* patior
* patefaciō, patefacere, patefēcī, patefactus – reveal
* pater, patris, m. – father
* patior, patī, passus sum – suffer, endure
* patrōnus, patrōnī, m. – patron
* paucī, paucae, pauca – few, a few
* paulīsper – for a short time
paulō – a little
* pauper, *gen.* pauperis – poor
* pavor, pavōris, m. – panic
* pāx, pācis, f. – peace
* pecūnia, pecūniae, f. – money
pedem *see* pēs
* pendeō, pendēre, pependī – hang
* per + *acc.* – through, along
percutiō, percutere, percussī, percussus – strike
* pereō, perīre, periī – die, perish
* perficiō, perficere, perfēcī, perfectus – finish
* perfidia, perfidiae, f. – treachery
* perfidus, perfida, perfidum – treacherous, untrustworthy
perfodiō, perfodere, perfōdī, perfossus – pick (teeth)
* perīculōsus, perīculōsa, perīculōsum – dangerous
* perīculum, perīculī, n. – danger
periī *see* pereō
perītē – skilfully
* perītus, perīta, perītum – skilful
* permōtus, permōta, permōtum – alarmed, disturbed
perpetuus, perpetua, perpetuum – perpetual
in perpetuum – for ever
perscrūtor, perscrūtārī, perscrūtātus sum – examine
perstō, perstāre, perstitī – persist
* persuādeō, persuādēre, persuāsī, – persuade
perterreō, perterrēre, perterruī, perterritus – terrify
* perterritus, perterrita, perterritum – terrified

perturbō, perturbāre, perturbāvī, perturbātus – disturb, alarm
* perveniō, pervenīre, pervēnī – reach, arrive at
* pēs, pedis, m. – foot, paw
pedem referre – step back
pessimus *see* malus
* pestis, pestis, f. – pest, scoundrel
petauristārius, petauristāriī, m. – acrobat
* petō, petere, petīvī, petītus – make for, attack; seek, beg for, ask for
philosopha, philosophae, f. – (female) philosopher
philosophia, philosophiae, f. – philosophy
philosophus, philosophī, m. – philosopher
pīpiō, pīpiāre, pīpiāvī – chirp
* placet, placēre, placuit – please, suit
* plaudō, plaudere, plausī, plausus – applaud, clap
* plaustrum, plaustrī, n. – wagon, cart
plausus, plausūs, m. – applause
* plēnus, plēna, plēnum – full
plērīque, plēraeque, plēraque – most
pluit, pluere, pluit – rain
plūrimus, plūs *see* multus
* pōculum, pōculī, n. – wine-cup
* poena, poenae, f. – punishment
* poenās dare – pay the penalty, be punished
* poēta, poētae, m. – poet
polliceor, pollicērī, pollicitus sum – promise
polyspaston, polyspastī, n. – crane
* pompa, pompae, f. – procession
* pōnō, pōnere, posuī, positus – put, place, put up
* pōns, pontis, m. – bridge
pontifex, pontificis, m. – priest
Pontifex Maximus – Chief Priest
poposcī *see* poscō
* populus, populī, m. – people
porrigō, porrigere, porrēxī, porrēctus – stretch out
* porta, portae, f. – gate

porticus, porticūs, f. – colonnade
* portō, portāre, portāvī, portātus –
　carry
* portus, portūs, m. – harbour
* poscō, poscere, poposcī – demand,
　ask for
positus *see* pōnō
possideō, possidēre, possēdī,
　possessus – possess
* possum, posse, potuī – can, be able
* post +*acc.* – after, behind
* posteā – afterwards
posterī, posterōrum, m.pl. –
　future generations, posterity
postīcum, postīcī, n. – back gate
* postquam – after, when
* postrēmō – finally, lastly
* postrīdiē – on the next day
* postulō, postulāre, postulāvī,
　postulātus – demand
posuī *see* pōnō
* potēns, *gen.* potentis – powerful
potes *see* possum
* potestās, potestātis, f. – power
potius – rather
potuī *see* possum
* praebeō, praebēre, praebuī,
　praebitus – provide
* praeceps, *gen.* praecipitis – headlong
praecipitō, praecipitāre, praecipitāvī
　– hurl
* praecō, praecōnis, m. – herald,
　announcer
praedīcō, praedīcere, praedīxī,
　praedictus – foretell, predict
* praeficiō, praeficere, praefēcī,
　praefectus – put in charge
* praemium, praemiī, n. – prize,
　reward, profit
praeruptus, praerupta, praeruptum –
　sheer, steep
praesēns, *gen.* praesentis –
　present, ready
praesertim – especially
* praesidium, praesidiī, n. – protection
* praestō, praestāre, praestitī – show,
　display

* praesum, praeesse, praefuī – be in
　charge of
praeter +*acc.* – except
* praetereā – besides
* praetereō, praeterīre, praeteriī –
　pass by, go past
praetextus, praetexta, praetextum –
　with a purple border
praetōriānus, praetōriānī, m. –
　praetorian (member of
　emperor's bodyguard)
praetōrius, praetōria, praetōrium –
　praetorian
　ōrnāmenta praetōria – honorary
　praetorship, honorary rank of
　praetor
* prāvus, prāva, prāvum – evil
* precēs, precum, f.pl. – prayers
* precor, precārī, precātus sum –
　pray (to)
* pretiōsus, pretiōsa, pretiōsum –
　expensive, precious
* pretium, pretiī, n. – price
prīmō – at first
prīmum – first
* prīmus, prīma, prīmum – first
　in prīmā parte – in the forefront
* prīnceps, prīncipis, m. – chief,
　chieftain
* prīncipia, prīncipiōrum, n.pl. –
　headquarters
* prior – first, in front
* prius – earlier
* priusquam – before, until
* prō +*abl.* – in front of, for, in return
　for
probus, proba, probum – honest
procāx, *gen.* procācis – impudent,
　impolite
* prōcēdō, prōcēdere, prōcessī –
　advance, proceed
* procul – far off
* prōcumbō, prōcumbere, prōcubuī –
　fall down
* proficīscor, proficīscī, profectus sum
　– set out

*prōgredior, prōgredī, prōgressus sum
   – advance
prohibeō, prohibēre, prohibuī,
   prohibitus – prevent
*prōmittō, prōmittere, prōmīsī,
   prōmissus – promise
prōnūntiō, prōnūntiāre, prōnūntiāvī,
   prōnūntiātus – proclaim, preach
*prope – near
prophēta, prophētae, m. – prophet
prōpōnō, prōpōnere, prōposuī,
   prōpositus – propose, put
   forward
prōsiliō, prōsilīre, prōsiluī – leap
   forward, jump
prōspectus, prōspectūs, m. – view
prōspiciō, prōspicere, prōspexī –
   look out
*prōvincia, prōvinciae, f. – province

*proximus, proxima, proximum –
   nearest, next to
*prūdentia, prūdentiae, f. – prudence,
   good sense, shrewdness
psittacus, psittacī, m. – parrot
*pūblicus, pūblica, pūblicum – public
*puella, puellae, f. – girl
*puer, puerī, m. – boy
*pugna, pugnae, f. – fight
*pugnō, pugnāre, pugnāvī – fight
*pulcher, pulchra, pulchrum –
   beautiful
*pulsō, pulsāre, pulsāvī, pulsātus –
   hit, knock at, thump, punch
pulvīnus, pulvīnī, m. – cushion
pūmiliō, pūmiliōnis, m. – dwarf
*pūniō, pūnīre, pūnīvī, pūnītus –
   punish
pūrus, pūra, pūrum – pure, clean,
   spotless
pyra, pyrae, f. – pyre

q

*quadrāgintā – forty
quaedam *see* quīdam
*quaerō, quaerere, quaesīvī, quaesītus
   – search for, look for
*quālis, quāle – what sort of
   tālis . . . quālis – such . . . as
*quam – (1) how
   quam celerrimē – as quickly as
   possible
*quam – (2) than
*quamquam – although
quandō – when
*quantus, quanta, quantum – how big
*quārē? – why?
*quārtus, quārta, quārtum – fourth
*quasi – as if
*quattuor – four
*-que – and
quendam *see* quīdam
*quī, quae, quod – who, which
*quia – because
*quicquam (*also spelt* quidquam) –
   anything

quid? *see* quis?
*quīdam, quaedam, quoddam – one,
   a certain
quidem – indeed
   nē . . . quidem – not even
*quiēs, quiētis, f. – rest
quiēscō, quiēscere, quiēvī – rest
*quīnquāgintā – fifty
*quīnque – five
*quīntus, quīnta, quīntum – fifth
*quis? quid? – who? what?
   quid vīs? – what do you want?
quisque, quaeque, quidque – each
   one
   optimus quisque – all the best
   people
*quō? – where? where to?
*quō modō? – how? in what way?
*quod – because
*quondam – one day, once
*quoque – also, too
*quot? – how many?
quotannīs – every year

r

* rapiō, rapere, rapuī, raptus – seize, grab
raptim – hastily, quickly
* ratiōnēs, ratiōnum, f.pl. – accounts
ratiōnēs subdūcere – draw up accounts, write up accounts
rē *see* rēs
rebellō, rebellāre, rebellāvī – rebel, revolt
rēbus *see* rēs
* recipiō, recipere, recēpī, receptus – recover, take back
sē recipere – recover
recitō, recitāre, recitāvī, recitātus – recite, read out
rēctē – rightly, properly
* recumbō, recumbere, recubuī – lie down, recline
* recūsō, recūsāre, recūsāvī, recūsātus – refuse
* reddō, reddere, reddidī, redditus – give back, make
redēmptor, redēmptōris, m. – contractor, builder
* redeō, redīre, rediī – return, go back, come back
redeundum est vōbīs – you must return
* redūcō, redūcere, redūxī, reductus – lead back
* referō, referre, rettulī, relātus – bring back, carry, deliver, tell, report
pedem referre – step back
* reficiō, reficere, refēcī, refectus – repair
* rēgīna, rēgīnae, f. – queen
rēgnō, rēgnāre, rēgnāvī – reign
* rēgnum, rēgnī, n. – kingdom
* regredior, regredī, regressus sum – go back, return
relēgō, relēgāre, relēgāvī, relēgātus – exile
* relinquō, relinquere, relīquī, relictus – leave

reliquus, reliqua, reliquum – remaining
rem *see* rēs
* remedium, remediī, n. – cure
remittō, remittere, remīsī, remissus – send back
repetō, repetere, repetīvī, repetītus – claim
rēpō, rēpere, rēpsī – crawl
* rēs, reī, f. – thing, business
* rē vērā – in fact, truly, really
rem administrāre – manage the task
rem cōgitāre – consider the problem
rem cōnficere – finish the job
rem nārrāre – tell the story
rem perficere – finish the job
rērum status – situation, state of affairs
* rēs adversae – misfortune
resignō, resignāre, resignāvī, resignātus – open, unseal
* resistō, resistere, restitī – resist
respiciō, respicere, respexī – look at, look upon
* respondeō, respondēre, respondī – reply
respōnsum, respōnsī, n. – answer
resurgō, resurgere, resurrēxī – rise again
* retineō, retinēre, retinuī, retentus – keep, hold back
retrō – back
rettulī *see* referō
* reveniō, revenīre, revēnī – come back, return
* revertor, revertī, reversus sum – turn back, return
revocō, revocāre, revocāvī, revocātus – recall, call back
* rēx, rēgis, m. – king
rhētor, rhētoris, m. – teacher
* rīdeō, rīdēre, rīsī – laugh, smile
* rīpa, rīpae, f. – river bank

* rogō, rogāre, rogāvī, rogātus – ask
Rōma, Rōmae, f. – Rome
Rōmae – at Rome
Rōmānī, Rōmānōrum, m.pl. –
Romans
Rōmānus, Rōmāna, Rōmānum –
Roman
rosa, rosae, f. – rose

rumpō, rumpere, rūpī, ruptus –
break, split
* ruō, ruere, ruī – rush
rūpēs, rūpis, f. – rock, crag
rūrī – in the country
* rūrsus – again
rūsticus, rūstica, rūsticum – country,
in the country
vīlla rūstica – house in the country

S

saccārius, saccāriī, m. – docker,
dock-worker
* sacer, sacra, sacrum – sacred
* sacerdōs, sacerdōtis, m. – priest
sacerdōtium, sacerdōtiī, n. –
priesthood
sacrificium, sacrificiī, n. – offering,
sacrifice
sacrificō, sacrificāre, sacrificāvī,
sacrificātus – sacrifice
* saepe – often
* saeviō, saevīre, saeviī – be in a rage
* saevus, saeva, saevum – savage, cruel
* saltō, saltāre, saltāvī – dance
* salūs, salūtis, f. – safety, health
salūtātiō, salūtātiōnis, f. – the
morning visit
* salūtō, salūtāre, salūtāvī, salūtātus –
greet
* salvē! – hello!
* sānē – obviously
* sanguis, sanguinis, m. – blood
sānō, sānāre, sānāvī, sānātus – heal,
cure, treat
* sapiēns, *gen.* sapientis – wise
sarcinae, sarcinārum, f.pl. – bags,
luggage
* satis – enough
* saxum, saxī, n. – rock
scaena, scaenae, f. – stage, scene
scālae, scālārum, f.pl. – ladders
* scelestus, scelesta, scelestum –
wicked
* scelus, sceleris, n. – crime
scīlicet – obviously

* scindō, scindere, scidī, scissus – tear,
tear up, cut up, cut open, carve
* scio, scīre, scīvī – know
* scrībō, scrībere, scrīpsī, scrīptus –
write
sculpō, sculpere, sculpsī, sculptus –
model, carve
* sē – himself, herself, themselves
sēcum – with him, with her, with
them
* secō, secāre, secuī, sectus – cut
* secundus, secunda, secundum –
second
secūris, secūris, f. – axe
secūtus *see* sequor
* sed – but
* sedeō, sedēre, sēdī – sit
* sēdēs, sēdis, f. – seat
* sella, sellae, f. – chair
* semper – always
* senātor, senātōris, m. – senator
senectūs, senectūtis, f. – old age
* senex, senis, m. – old man
* sententia, sententiae, f. – opinion
* sentiō, sentīre, sēnsī, sēnsus – feel,
notice
* septem – seven
* septimus, septima, septimum –
seventh
* septuāgintā – seventy
* sepulcrum, sepulcrī, n. – tomb
* sequor, sequī, secūtus sum – follow
sequēns, *gen.* sequentis – following
* serēnus, serēna, serēnum – calm, clear
* sermō, sermōnis, m. – conversation

* serviō, servīre, servīvī – serve (as a slave)
servitūs, servitūtis, f. – slavery
* servō, servāre, servāvī, servātus – save, look after
fidem servāre – keep a promise, keep faith
* servus, servī, m. – slave
sēstertius, sēstertiī, m. – sesterce (coin)
sēstertium vīciēns – two million sesterces
sevērē – severely
* sevērus, sevēra, sevērum – severe, strict
* sex – six
* sexāgintā – sixty
* sextus, sexta, sextum – sixth
* sī – if
sibi *see* sē
* sīc – thus, in this way
* sīcut – like
* signum, signī, n. – sign, seal, signal
* silentium, silentiī, n. – silence
sileō, silēre, siluī – be silent
* silva, silvae, f. – wood
simul – at the same time
* simulac, simulatque – as soon as
* sine +*abl.* – without
situs, sita, situm – situated
* sōl, sōlis, m. – sun
sōlācium, sōlāciī, n. – comfort
* soleō, solēre – be accustomed
* sollicitus, sollicita, sollicitum – worried, anxious
* sōlus, sōla, sōlum – alone, lonely, only, on one's own
* solvō, solvere, solvī, solūtus – loosen, untie, cast off
* sonitus, sonitūs, m. – sound
* sordidus, sordida, sordidum – dirty
* soror, sorōris, f. – sister
* sors, sortis, f. – lot
sorte ductus – chosen by lot
spargō, spargere, sparsī, sparsus – scatter

* spectāculum, spectāculī, n. – show, spectacle
spectātor, spectātōris, m. – spectator
* spectō, spectāre, spectāvī, spectātus – look at, watch
specus, specūs, m. – cave
* spernō, spernere, sprēvī, sprētus – despise, reject
* spērō, spērāre, spērāvī – hope, expect
* spēs, speī, f. – hope
spīna, spīnae, f. – thorn, toothpick
splendidus, splendida, splendidum – splendid, impressive
sportula, sportulae, f. – handout
stābam *see* stō
* statim – at once
* statiō, statiōnis, f. – post
statua, statuae, f. – statue
statūra, statūrae, f. – height
status, statūs, m. – state
rērum status – situation, state of affairs
stēlla, stēllae, f. – star
sternō, sternere, strāvī, strātus – lay low
* stō, stāre, stetī – stand, lie at anchor
Stōicus, Stōicī, m. – Stoic (believer in Stoic philosophy)
* stola, stolae, f. – dress
* strēnuē – hard, energetically
* strepitus, strepitūs, m. – noise, din
stultitia, stultitiae, f. – stupidity, foolishness
* stultus, stulta, stultum – stupid, foolish
* suāvis, suāve – sweet
* suāviter – sweetly
* sub +*abl.* – under, beneath
subdūcō, subdūcere, subdūxī, subductus – draw up
ratiōnēs subdūcere – draw up accounts, write up accounts
* subitō – suddenly
sublātus *see* tollō
subscrībō, subscrībere, subscrīpsī, subscrīptus – sign

* subveniō, subvenīre, subvēnī – help,
  come to help
suffīgō, suffīgere, suffīxī, suffīxus –
  nail, fasten
* sum, esse, fuī – be
  estō! – be!
* summus, summa, summum –
  highest, greatest, top
* sūmptuōsus, sūmptuōsa,
  sūmptuōsum – expensive,
  lavish, costly
superbē – arrogantly
* superbus, superba, superbum –
  arrogant, proud
* superō, superāre, superāvī, superātus
  – overcome, overpower

superstes, superstitis, m. – survivor
* supersum, superesse, superfuī –
  survive
* surgō, surgere, surrēxī – get up, rise
* suscipiō, suscipere, suscēpī,
  susceptus – undertake, take on
suspīciō, suspīciōnis, f. – suspicion
suspīciōsus, suspīciōsa,
  suspīciōsum – suspicious
* suspicor, suspicārī, suspicātus sum –
  suspect
* suus, sua, suum – his, her, their,
  his own
suī, suōrum, m.pl. – his men, his
  family, their families

t

T. = Titus
* taberna, tabernae, f. – shop, inn
* taceō, tacēre, tacuī – be silent,
  be quiet
* tacitē – quietly, silently
* tacitus, tacita, tacitum – quiet, silent,
  in silence
* taedet, taedēre – be tiring
  mē taedet – I am tired, I am bored
* tālis, tāle – such
  tālis . . . quālis – such . . . as
* tam – so
* tamen – however
* tamquam – as, like
* tandem – at last
  tangō, tangere, tetigī, tāctus – touch
* tantum – only
* tantus, tanta, tantum – so great, such
  a great
  tapēte, tapētis, n. – tapestry
  tardē – late
  tardius – too late
* tardus, tarda, tardum – late
  taurus, taurī, m. – bull
  tē see tū
* tēctum, tēctī, n. – ceiling, roof
  tēgula, tēgulae, f. – tile

temperāns, *gen.* temperantis –
  temperate, self-controlled
* tempestās, tempestātis, f. – storm
* templum, templī, n. – temple
* temptō, temptāre, temptāvī,
  temptātus – try, put to the test
* tempus, temporis, n. – time
* tenebrae, tenebrārum, f.pl. –
  darkness
* teneō, tenēre, tenuī, tentus – hold
* tergum, tergī, n. – back
* terra, terrae, f. – ground, land
  orbis terrārum – world
* terreō, terrēre, terruī, territus –
  frighten
  terribilis, terribile – terrible
* tertius, tertia, tertium – third
* testāmentum, testāmentī, n. – will
* testis, testis, m.f. – witness
  theātrum, theātrī, n. – theatre
  Tiberis, Tiberis, m. – river Tiber
  tibi see tū
  tībia, tībiae, f. – pipe
  tībiīs cantāre – play on the pipes
  tībīcen, tībīcinis, m. – pipe player
  tignum, tignī, n. – beam
* timeō, timēre, timuī – be afraid, fear

timidē – fearfully
timidus, timida, timidum – fearful,
  frightened
* timor, timōris, m. – fear
titulus, titulī, m. – notice, slogan,
  inscription, label
toga, togae, f. – toga
* tollō, tollere, sustulī, sublātus – raise,
  lift up, hold up
* tot – so many
* tōtus, tōta, tōtum – whole
* trādō, trādere, trādidī, trāditus –
  hand over
* trahō, trahere, trāxī, tractus – drag
tranquillē – peacefully
* trānseō, trānsīre, trānsiī – cross
trānsfīgō, trānsfīgere, trānsfīxī,
  trānsfīxus – pierce
trānsiliō, trānsilīre, trānsiluī – jump
  through

* trēs, tria – three
* tribūnus, tribūnī, m. – tribune
  (high-ranking officer)
trīciēns sēstertium – three million
  sesterces
triclīnium, triclīniī, n. – dining-room
* trīgintā – thirty
* trīstis, trīste – sad
* tū, tuī – you (singular)
* tuba, tubae, f. – trumpet
tubicen, tubicinis, m. – trumpeter
* tum – then
  tum dēmum – then at last, only
  then
* turba, turbae, f. – crowd
* tūtus, tūta, tūtum – safe
* tuus, tua, tuum – your (singular),
  yours
Tyrius, Tyria, Tyrium – Tyrian
  (coloured with dye from city
  of Tyre)

u

* ubi – where, when
* ubīque – everywhere
ulcīscor, ulcīscī, ultus sum – take
  revenge on
* ultimus, ultima, ultimum – furthest,
  last
* ultiō, ultiōnis, f. – revenge
* umbra, umbrae, f. – shadow, ghost
* umerus, umerī, m. – shoulder
* umquam – ever
  ūnā cum +abl. – together with
* unda, undae, f. – wave
* unde – from where
* undique – on all sides

* ūnus, ūna, ūnum – one
urbānus, urbāna, urbānum – smart,
  fashionable
* urbs, urbis, f. – city
usquam – anywhere
usque ad +acc. – right up to
* ut – (1) as
* ut – (2) that, so that, in order that
* ūtilis, ūtile – useful
* utrum – whether
  utrum . . . an – whether . . . or
  utrum . . . necne – whether . . .
  or not
* uxor, uxōris, f. – wife

v

vacuus, vacua, vacuum – empty
* valdē – very much, very
* valē – goodbye, farewell
valedīcō, valedīcere, valedīxī – say
  goodbye

valētūdō, valētūdinis, f. – health
validus, valida, validum – strong
* vehementer – violently, loudly
* vehō, vehere, vexī, vectus – carry

*vel – or
vel . . . vel – either . . . or
velim, vellem *see* volō
vēnālīcius, vēnālīciī, m. –
slave-dealer
* vēnātiō, vēnātiōnis, f. – hunt
* vēndō, vēndere, vēndidī, vēnditus –
sell
* venēnum, venēnī, n. – poison
* venia, veniae, f. – mercy
* veniō, venīre, vēnī – come
venter, ventris, m. – stomach
* ventus, ventī, m. – wind
Venus, Veneris, f. – Venus (goddess
of love)
verber, verberis, n. – blow
* verberō, verberāre, verberāvī,
verberātus – strike, beat
* verbum, verbī, n. – word
versus, versa, versum – having turned
versus, versūs, m. – verse, line of
poetry
* vertō, vertere, vertī, versus – turn
* vērum, vērī, n. – truth
* vērus, vēra, vērum – true, real
*   rē vērā – in fact, truly, really
* vester, vestra, vestrum – your
(plural)
* vestīmenta, vestīmentōrum, n.pl. –
clothes
vestrum *see* vōs
vetus, *gen.* veteris – old
* vexō, vexāre, vexāvī, vexātus –
annoy
vī *see* vīs
* via, viae, f. – street, way
vīciēns sēstertium – two million
sesterces
victima, victimae, f. – victim
* victor, victōris, m. – victor, winner
victōria, victōriae, f. – victory
victus *see* vincere

* videō, vidēre, vīdī, vīsus – see
videor, vidērī, vīsus sum – seem
vigilō, vigilāre, vigilāvī – stay awake
* vīgintī – twenty
* vīlla, vīllae, f. – house, villa
* vinciō, vincīre, vīnxī, vīnctus – bind,
tie up
* vincō, vincere, vīcī, victus – conquer,
win, be victorious
* vīnum, vīnī, n. – wine
* vir, virī, m. – man
vīrēs, vīrium, f.pl – strength
virgō, virginis, f. – virgin
* virtūs, virtūtis, f. – courage
vīs, f. – force, violence
vīsitō, vīsitāre, vīsitāvī, vīsitātus –
visit
vīsus *see* videō
* vīta, vītae, f. – life
vītam agere – lead a life
vitium, vitiī, n. – sin
* vītō, vītāre, vītāvī, vītātus – avoid
* vituperō, vituperāre, vituperāvī,
vituperātus – blame, curse
* vīvō, vīvere, vīxī – live, be alive
* vīvus, vīva, vīvum – alive, living
* vix – hardly, scarcely, with difficulty
vōbīs *see* vōs
vōcem *see* vōx
* vocō, vocāre, vocāvī, vocātus – call
* volō, velle, voluī – want
quid vīs? – what do you want?
velim – I should like
* volvō, volvere, volvī, volūtus – turn
*   in animō volvere – wonder, turn
over in the mind
* vōs – you (plural)
vōbīscum – with you (plural)
* vōx, vōcis, f. – voice
* vulnerō, vulnerāre, vulnerāvī,
vulnerātus – wound, injure
* vulnus, vulneris, n. – wound
* vultus, vultūs, m. – expression, face